# Life Is a Story

Ernestine Meadows May

authorHOUSE®

*AuthorHouse™*
*1663 Liberty Drive*
*Bloomington, IN 47403*
*www.authorhouse.com*
*Phone: 1-800-839-8640*

*© 2009 Ernestine Meadows May. All rights reserved.*

*No part of this book may be reproduced, stored in a retrieval system, or transmitted by any means without the written permission of the author.*

*First published by AuthorHouse 12/22/2009*

*ISBN: 978-1-4389-5369-4 (sc)*
*ISBN: 978-1-4389-5370-0 (hc)*

*Library of Congress Control Number: 2009908821*

*Printed in the United States of America*
*Bloomington, Indiana*

*This book is printed on acid-free paper.*

# Dedication

Mary Franklin Meadows

*Ernestine Meadows May is married to Floyd May and presently reside in Gary, Indiana and Las Vegas, Nevada. They have four children; Andre, Don, Kelly, and Mona. Five grandchildren; Andreona, Andre Jr., Dominique, Kennedy, and Makayla.*

This memoir is dedicated to the memory of my parents, Jessie Hall Meadows-Sanders and Arthur Meadows (my father who did not live to witness my birth); Earl Hall, my grandfather; my grandmother, Mary Franklin Meadows; Homer Sanders, my stepfather, and to all who have crossed the bar before me; my oldest sisters, Mary Alice Meadows-McNeal and Arther Mae Meadows-Gray; my brother,

Robert E. Meadows; my stepsister, Emma Jean Houston; my surrogate grandfather, Wylie "Bud" Leonard; my uncle and aunt, Frank and Hilda Meadows; Boogie and Lynn Saxton, our neighbors; my dear friend, whom I will always hold dear to my heart, Fannie Wilson; and especially to all my great ancestors who paid the price for me being here, free, with their spirit still in me. I especially dedicate this book to my grandchildren, great-grandchildren, and my only surviving aunt, Tressie K. Hall, and as far as this bloodline is blessed to continue.

# Acknowledgment

Thank you, Dion Harding, for inspiring me to do what I've always had in my heart to do: write my story!

I give a very sincere appreciation to Floyd May, my husband, for his support during all my life's little projects.

# Table of Contents

| | |
|---|---|
| Dedication | v |
| Acknowledgment | vii |
| Introduction | xi |
| Childhood Times | 1 |
| A Very Special Holiday | 11 |
| A Time to Be Happy and a Time to Be Sad | 15 |
| Home Work Ethics | 19 |
| Recreation and Community Relations | 31 |
| Segregation vs. Integration | 35 |
| Morals and Values | 41 |
| Early School to College Days | 51 |
| My Career Development | 67 |
| Reflections | 73 |
| Epilogue | 81 |
| A Poem of Freedom | 83 |

# Introduction

Autumn is a fantastic time of year! It lends itself to sunny days, crisp cool air, bright skies, and the painted greens of autumn. You just can't beat that. Akin to this very euphoric thrill, is the fact of being retired and sitting on an Amtrak Eagle to San Antonio, Texas. I chose this mode of transportation just because I now live the easy life. No more worries about tomorrow's work. I am in the now moment, and it feels so good.

This day is so perfect that I am inspired to begin to write this book, as I have promised to do upon my retirement. The train is beginning to move outside Union Station in Chicago so slowly and so very quietly, as if she speaks to me of peace, and a deep appreciation of life arouses my senses to challenge the inner sanctions of my thoughts.

This train trip is nothing like the one my sister and I first took when I was about nine years old and Augustine, my sister, was eleven years old. We were returning from a trip that we had made to Chicago with my oldest sister, Mary, and her family. They had spent a week with us in Biscoe, Arkansas, as part of their summer vacation. Mum had allowed us to visit with them for a week, and we also visited with Uncle

Earsel, Mum's brother, the last two days of the trip. At the end of the week, Earsel put us on the train for home. Leaving from Union Station in Chicago should have been a little scary but not so. Kids could ride the train without adult supervision back in the day, because it would be expected that other traveling adults would look out for the likes of us as we traveled. No harm, no foul!

Anyway, I lost my ticket just a matter of minutes after getting on the train. A few miles outside the station, I could hear the porter yell out, "Have your tickets ready." I immediately went into a panic mode, because I knew not where my ticket was. This ticket was our legal tender for traveling to Arkansas.

My aunt, Marcella, had packed a lunch for our trip, and I was too busy eating all the goodies almost before we had left from the station. Inadvertently, I had thrown the ticket, along with the candy wrappers, into the garbage. I asked an attendant on the train what would happen if a person was riding the train without a ticket, and he replied, "They will just throw the person off the train at the next stop." I was really beginning to panic then. I started retracing my steps, and just before the conductor reached our seating area, I made a dash to the garbage can at the end of the car, dug in, and voilà, I found the candy wrapper and the ticket crumpled together. Just in time. Thank God I didn't have to be thrown off the train!

My motivation for writing this memoir is to leave with my grandchildren and great-grandchildren some semblance of family history, tradition, custom, and legacy. Hopefully, others reading this story will also be inspired to know that, by the grace of God, anyone can overcome the issues of life, rise to the occasion, and live a great life.

It was a very interesting era (I call it the era of *being*). If you lived, loved, and still experienced the things of my generation during this period, you would understand the state of being just a bit more.

This is my testimony of life as I experienced it at a time when segregation in the South was making way for a more desired term: "integration." It was a time when bigotry needed to be exposed, constitutional laws needed to pertain to blacks as well as all citizens, and education needed to be compulsory for every child. On the other hand, we were able to witness the birth of rock and roll, poodle skirts, bell-bottom pants, petticoats, ponytails, the love generation, VW Bugs, Sputnik, and Elvis Presley's debut on the *Ed Sullivan Show*. (Imagine that people tried to have him banned from television because he wiggled his legs in a much too provocative way.)

We went from using oil lamps to electric lights, from wood heat to butane, from an ice box to a refrigerator, from listening to radio to watching TV, from writing letters to using a rotary telephone, from down on the farm to uptown, from pigtails to ponytails. Progress came very slowly in the South; *change* came even more slowly!

I now have four children of my own, and from time to time, I would try to share some of my experiences with them relative to my childhood, contrasting and comparing behaviors of the different times. A world of very interesting differences when you compare today's standards and behaviors with those of the past. When my kids had listened too many times to stories of my childhood, they would begin to shudder, "Not again!" So now, I'm telling my story to a different audience, hopefully an audience who has an ear to hear it. I also anticipate that my grandchildren and great-grandchildren will relish the memories of this grandparent, who stepped to "the beat of a different drummer" and carved out a route for herself from a nondescript farmer's daughter to a life enriched with dreams attained!

My childhood is a very memorable one to me. I am amazed that the recollections of my youth are so very vivid and clear that it seems as though they happened just a few years ago. I can almost even smell the roses that were growing in Mrs. Thedonia McDonald's front yard as I passed her house on a summer Sunday morning on my way to church. We were sure to get a red rose from her on Mother's Day to indicate my mum was still living, and she'd give my mum a white one because her mum had passed. The more I activate my memory to recall the facts of my childhood days, the more I remember the tiny details and minuscule experiences.

My earliest memory finds me sitting in bed with my mum in the living/bedroom. It felt good and safe there. Security was not a word that I was aware of, but it describes best how I see it now. From infancy to about four years old, children usually slept in bed with their parents, because of the limited space in homes and the large family nucleus, hence, the dual functionality of living and sleeping spaces. I was about four years old at this time, because I had not enrolled in school yet. I remember I was anxiously anticipating becoming six years old so that I could attend school with my siblings.

We lived on the property located in Biscoe, Arkansas, called the OdomPlace. It was named because of the owner, Ms. Helen Odom. Most plantations were so named because of the owner.

Ms. Odom was the high school math teacher in Biscoe. I always thought Ms. Odom must have been the richest woman in the world. I never dreamed that one day, I would perhaps become a property owner, landlord, and rise to the level of success that she had. My mother and stepfather sharecropped her farmland. Each farm had living quarters for the family. Sharecropping meant that for whatever crops our family harvested, Ms. Odom, the landowner, would get 50 or 60 percent of the profits, depending on the prearranged contract. It was a contract that was given by word. A person's word was all that was needed for the bond. This arrangement allowed us to live on the property and receive a line of credit, backed by Ms. Odom, for purchases made at Betzner's store with the promise to pay all debts when the crops were in at harvest time.

I loved the Odom's Place, because it held some very good times for my siblings and me. I had two brothers and five sisters. I am the youngest of the seven children. Two of my oldest sisters had already reached the age of responsibility and had gone to Memphis to live with Aunt Essie and work with her at the Peabody Hotel.

Reminiscing is a good thing when it allows you to relive some of the good old days you had as a child. I don't think I would change anything about my past. Well, maybe a few things! Sure, there were one or two embarrassing moments for me as I grew older, and I suppose that I desired to have some of the things that we could not afford, but as long as I was a child, I didn't even miss those things, because I had not been exposed to them. In the end, I know that everything that has happened to/for me happened in order to make me the person that I am today. Life has changed, I haven't! As hard as my life seemed to me at the time, I know my mum did all that she knew how to do with the resources available to her and the limited education that she had. I was never embarrassed because of her. One would never guess that she had only attended grade school.

During the early years of my life, I remember cotton being the most important staple of our livelihood. My stepfather planted, we chopped and weeded, and in the fall, we picked the fluffy stuff. The bolls that held the cotton had sharp pricks that would scratch our hands when the cotton was pulled from the ripened fruit. Greater than scarred hands for life, was the fact that cotton deprived us from being in our rightful places in school from September to November. And in the spring, around April and May, again we had to attend to the tender growths in the fields. So do the math; our time in school was four out of the nine months of school. I often wonder where the child labor laws were back then. If the local, state, and federal government had been paying attention, we could have been freed from that hardship and would have been allowed to attend school as our white counterparts.

Also, why wasn't the State Department of Education checking to see why most of the black students were not regularly attending school? Seems like a plot to me!

I'm sure we helped to cheat ourselves by having a school administration that did not properly report our absenteeism, because it would mean a cut in state funding for our school. So yes, records were padded. There was no accountability and no one to advocate for us! The school administration knew that most families in our area, as well as other outlying areas, depended on children helping the family to harvest crops for their livelihood. Parents, for the most part, did not receive an education past the fifth grade. Some had not attended school at all. I will not go into the history of post slavery oppressions and mentalities.

The school administration did us a disservice by accommodating the situation rather than affecting change in the system that could allow parents to profit through farming and children could benefit through attending school nine months of the year. A federal and state bailout for education at that time perhaps could have made a profound effect on our economy's stability and well-being in sustaining our nation's power. It is possible that as blacks, we would now be on a more equal playing field. Quite possibly some of the things playing out in our economy would have much less fallout at this time. Much healing could have been done between black/white relations.

Most kids like me had the drive to finish high school and move on to another state or region to seek employment outside of chopping and picking cotton. There was always this stigma that prospective job applicants had a greater edge because of a better educational background.

I later found out that my meager five to six out of nine months of early education sometimes surpassed my counterparts in many cases of higher education and also in the job and career market. I think my drive to succeed came from my mum. I now realize that she learned from us bringing home our schoolwork, and her determination to make the best of what she could do worked for our family. Now, this proves to me that, in most instances, quality played out over quantity.

# Childhood Times

As kids, my siblings and I were very inventive when it came to play and recreation. Today's kids want it all; parents give too much. The making of one's character is developed by a lack, allowing the mind to create and invent in the absence of what one does not have.

A fun day for me was to play with my paper dolls cut out from a Sears and Roebuck catalog. There were many clothes to choose for them from the catalog. My sister and I would play paper dolls for hours and hours on end. An old shoebox would house all the clothes and furnishings for several families.

I now watch my granddaughter play dolls electronically. She chooses her doll from a popular video program, clicks on the appropriate clothing to dress her, controls her shopping, and sets her up in a penthouse, all using the computer.

In the summertime, sprouts of long, green, ornamental grass became the model for practicing hair braiding. An early ear of corn could be a doll. We would dress it and put ribbons in the silk for its hair. A jump rope was made from plucking clover in the spring and intertwining the stems to make a long rope. Or we would make a crown of clover flowers for our heads. A Coke bottle was often used to make a doll. We would unwind the cords of a stiff, organic hemp rope cut to the desired length and place it inside the open end of the bottle for the hair.

A cutout picture of a girl would be glued to the opening of the bottle to make a more realistic human image. (Glue was made by mixing together flour and water to form a paste.)

My brothers made push wheelies by using the shiny tin lid of a molasses can and nailing it to the end of a board about three to five feet in length, and they would push it around and around the house, like a fun car race. We knew how to improvise. I think we invented the word ingenuity! They also made a wagon and a skateboard even before skateboards were in vogue. Wherever there were wheels and boards, something was created from them.

You see, we didn't know the meaning of the word "bored." It was never a word in our vocabulary. Overweight? We didn't have time to eat, because there was always something more interesting to do. There was no sitting around watching TV, playing videos, or eating pizza. Even if we had those things, we always preferred the out of doors, just having great fun!

As you read this, I would not want to send a double message that we were always working in the fields, so how could we find the time to play and have fun? As I stated before, fieldwork was for a season. There was a time to work and a time to play.

Coupled with putting together a life for my sisters and brothers, my mum also helped to raise three of her grandchildren—Joyce, Margaret, and Linda—in order to help out my older sisters so that they could become better established financially. Mum could never say no to anyone who needed her help.

When Joyce was a baby, she only had one bottle. One night, about midnight, she threw it down and broke it. Homer had to get out of bed, put on his clothes, walk about four miles to Mr. Betzner's house, and get him out of bed to open up his store to purchase a baby bottle. Joyce would not go to sleep without her bottle. She was not weaned from her bottle until she was five years old. She would do nothing without it. We would walk to church on Sunday morning with Joyce's bottle to her mouth. As we passed different houses, people would come out and laugh as they saw her pass by, walking and sucking on that bottle.

Margaret was always sickly. She constantly needed special attention. Mum did what needed to be done. She mostly relied on old-fashioned remedies that helped bring back Margaret's strength. She finally outgrew whatever problems she was having as a child.

My brothers were nice to our little nieces. They helped out with them without fussing or complaining. They were even nice to Stine and I. They built a playhouse for us in the fruit orchard.

My father had planted several peach, pear, apple, and plum trees before his death. They provided much shade for play and seclusion from an outside world. The orchard had become a gift to all of us from our father, though he was not able to witness the fruit of his labor. It was a place for respite and retreat! The playhouse was large enough to crawl into and sit down and play dolls all day long.

Bill and Jesse made and set a trap to catch a bird. They decided to take the trapped bird, dress it, and cook it over an open fire they built, just to see what it would taste like. I tasted it and found it not to be something I would put on my "favorite things to eat" list. Those brothers of mine would try anything when Mum was not around.

When our mum would go into town to do her errands, she left us alone with our oldest sister, Louise. Louise had her own things to do besides watching us. She would leave us alone to play as she began to cook dinner. That meant that she would need us to gather chips to make a fire in the cook stove. Most times, she would listen to her stories on radio for much too long and forget the fire in the stove. We'd have to start all over again, gathering more chips to get the fire going again. Her promise to us if we wouldn't rat her out to Mum would be to make us a batch of tea cakes. Oh yeah! We just loved her tea cakes, and she generally held true to her promise.

I remember the stories that Louise would listen to on radio during the day were *Stella Dallas* and *Our Girl Friday*. Her favorite position was with her ear glued to the side of the radio at the kitchen table. Later, in the evening, we would all listen to *Inner Sanctum*. Her music, *Boogy Blues*, came in at KOKY and WDIA radio stations. She just couldn't juggle listening to radio with other chores at the same time, but more times than not, dinner would be ready and on the table by the time Mum arrived home from the fields. A batch of tea cakes were always pleasing to the palate and offered forgiveness of all things undone! We gave her the nickname "Cakes" because of the tea cakes she would often bake for us.

Louise told us bedtime stories that were usually on the scary side. One in particular was "Johnny I Want my Liver Back." (You don't want to hear about it.) On a lighter note, there was the story of the headless man who walked aimlessly each night down the dark road that led from town to our house. There was a little bridge that crossed over a small brook; she said it was his favorite hangout. Each time I had to walk home alone at night from church, I thought about the headless man that I had been warned about. I almost swore I saw him coming toward me late one evening when I was in a hurry to get home early from church to do my homework. Her stories were always so grueling.

After hearing her bedtime stories, it took a long time for us to fall asleep for the night. It was comforting that Louise slept in the room with Stine and me, although she scared us out of our wits. Louise was always a good support for us kids.

My two older sisters, Mary Alice and Arther Mae, had left home and moved to Memphis to find a job. Emancipation happened at the age of eighteen.

Down the lane and at the edge of the little bridge was where our neighbor, Mr. Wright, had his village blacksmith shop. His kids were our friends. Sometimes, we would stop by his shop on our way home from school and watch him work from door's glance. We loved how he made the hot red irons flicker with fire each time he struck the irons with his hammer. It was always blazing hot inside his shop. I don't think he liked the idea of us being there. He seemed to be a very quiet and personal man, who was usually preoccupied and in deep thought. He certainly never hung out the welcome sign for us, if you know what I mean.

We were poor, and we didn't need any measurement by the USDA poverty guidelines to let us know that. However, we were very rich in so many areas. Our needs were always met, we were happy, we were a cohesive family, and we had no idea how the rest of the world lived. (We seemed normal to me, because everyone I knew lived as we did. Whites excluded. General observation allowed me that!) I don't know if we knew there was a rest of the world. I, at least, thought this was it! When I started school, I found out differently. That is what an education can do for you. Education is enlightenment; it opens your eyes and your entire being to many possibilities and realities.

I was always a thinker and a dreamer. The mind is a very complex and mysterious organ, and I sometimes wonder if dreaming is a means of escape. I believe also that it is a provoking mechanism. I sometimes dream of things that are not real, but I see those things as ideas, possibly to develop into future opportunities.

When we sadly moved from the Odom place, our next house was on the Robinson farm. Now we were closer to town and school. Our neighbors were the Tallys. They were good and decent white folks who had very playful grandchildren, Larry and Linda Jo, who would mostly visit their grandparents during the summer months.

Larry and Linda Jo became our playmates when they visited their grandparents. They would dash over to our house when they found out that kids close to their ages lived there. The biggest trouble we ever got into was when Linda Jo brought matches with her one day, and she decided we would set fire to the dry grass across the road from our house. As soon as she dropped the match, *swoosh*, it was gone. We tried to stomp out the fire, but the wind moved it out of control much too fast. Our brothers brought buckets of water and helped us to contain the fire. I thought, *Never again*. I'm sure Linda Jo was convinced as well.

There were great and positive things that came of our playing relationship. They taught us many group games, like Annie over, Red Rover, tag, hide-and-seek. We taught them Little Sally Walker, hopscotch, double Dutch, jacks, and London Bridge.

One of my favorites was a hide-and- seek game where we would chant and sing this tune:

Honey, honey bee baugh, I can't see y'all, last night and the night before, twenty-four robbers were at my door, I got up to let them in, but hit them in the head with the rollin' pin. How many licks did I give? 1, 2, 3, 4, 5, 6, 7, 8, 9, 10, ... [Counting continues to allow everyone to find hiding places.] Ready or not, here I come!

One day near the end of summer, Linda Jo brought over a beautiful picture that she had drawn and colored of a trip she and her family had taken to Arizona. There was a mountain in the center of the paper, with cactus and other plants indigenous to the territory. Birds and the hot sun were seen in the distance. It was a beautiful picture. I was almost there. This was another touch with the world outside that I had not experienced as yet. I didn't know how to look forward to the hopes and dreams to come. Looking at the picture seemed like a place too far away for me to ever visit.

Mrs. Tally's daughter, Elizabeth, helped us with many skills in math that we did not understand when we were in sixth grade. Fractions, decimals, long division, zeros in multiplication, and division, along with some complicated math reading problems. I am forever grateful to her for her time and patience with us. I have often used those skills in school and out. I think of Elizabeth and Ms. Odom's teachings of math and how those moments come back so vividly in my mind when I help my granddaughter, Dominique, with her homework. After Elizabeth helped us to finish our homework, we would stay over and watch TV until the ten o'clock news came on. Stine and I would then run home. Those evenings were a special treat!

*Love thy neighbor as thyself.*

My mum was limited in some of the modern techniques of canning foods, so she relied on the manual method, while our neighbor, Mrs. Tally, used the pressure cooker—until one day it exploded on her, and she was through with it. She brought it over to our house and said, "Here, Jessie, I'm done with this."

Mrs. Tally showed Mum the basics of the canning operation and left the contraption with her. Right away Mum began to use the cooker and, voilà, much success. Mum canned everything and anything. She even canned some vegetables and fruit for Mrs. Tally.

We always had great harvests of produce. There was plenty to provide our neighbors and friends with great bundles of a harvest. If there was one thing Mum and Homer did right, it was their ability to make great provisions for the family! We had more than enough with all the hogs, cows, pigs, and chickens that we raised. And if *that* was not enough, during hunting season, there was wild game, such as rabbits, squirrels, and deer. My mum would can most of the deer meat. She would soak the venison in saltwater and vinegar overnight to remove the "wild" taste. It made for a great, tender, pot roast.

Mum would store the fruit and vegetables that she canned in the pantry. Many times, we would open a jar of peaches and eat them, and Mum would not even miss them because she had so many. We had to eat the entire jar and dispose of the evidence, or she would know that we had invaded and raided the pantry. She took pride in making her jars of fruit and vegetables look as though they would be judged at the local county fair and would be awarded a blue ribbon for her entry. Her vegetable soup during the cold winter months was always a number-one hit with me! Pear preserves on a hot biscuit ran a second best!

We qualified for commodities that were issued monthly by the USDA. We received cheese, canned pork, rice, butter, meal, and flour. Mum became even more creative with her cooking. She added onions, green peppers, and other seasonings to the canned pork, simmered it, and poured it over rice, upgrading that dish to become a farmer's cuisine! More butter, more cakes, bread puddings, butter rolls, and cobblers, and the fact that Mum had a rich sweet tooth worked to our advantage. I regret that she did not write down some of her recipes to pass on to us.

As long as we lived at the Odom place, we hardly had any outside friends to play with, but for sure, we had each other. Lola, Maxine, Flo Catherine, L. C., Earlene, and Billy, our cousins, moved across the road from us for a short time, and we hooked up to play and had many fun times together.

I loved exploring the outer realms of our home to see what could be found through curious scavenger hunts. I once found a dumping ground near a stream of water about a half mile behind our house. Pieces of chipped and broken china, along with other finds, were used in our playhouse.

It was fun thinking of the family who perhaps lived at our house before we did and had used those items. It gave me a sense of connecting with others through imagination.

There was another area where I went on one of my scavenger hunts and found old Civil War relics, rustic bayonet guns, odd-looking canisters, and carved arrowhead rocks that probably had been used by Native Americans for hunting. I often thought about the circumstances behind these artifacts.

# A Very Special Holiday

Christmas was always a special time for us. Mum would begin baking cakes and pies at least three weeks in advance with the anticipation of the holiday season. The house would be filled with tantalizing aromas of cinnamon, coconut, vanilla, chocolate, and spices. We had candies and fruit that had a special way of filling the house with Christmas that I have not experience since childhood.

Buddy, my surrogate grandfather's son, sent his dad a package every year, and we could guess the exact contents every time: apples, oranges, and a variety of nuts and candies. Bud always turned the package over to Mum. What was it about apples and oranges that would fill the whole house with the blessed scents of Christmas? You just don't smell aromas throughout the house like that anymore.

I think Mum lived vicariously through us, as she had no memory of celebrating Christmas when she was a child. She really seemed to enjoy all the cooking, baking, and making Christmas a happy occasion for us.

Mum had made Christmas so special and important that I took it upon myself one year to go into the woods and retrieve the Christmas tree. I must have been about twelve or thirteen years old at the time. My brothers had the designated task to cut the tree each year, but they had left home by this time. No one else seemed as though they would be cutting the tree, and I was not going without a Christmas tree that year, or any other for that matter!

I remember walking miles across the fields to reach the woods. Walking alone, I encountered little rabbits and squirrels but no humans in my search for the right tree. I suppose I didn't have the good sense to be afraid at that age. Then again, we did not experience the same social problems that are prevalent in today's society.

I found small trees during my search. Most were too immature, some were lopsided, others were too skimpy, and there were large ones that were much too big for me. When I found the one that suited me, I chopped the trunk of the tree at its lowest point and hit it several times with the axe at an angle. This was the way I had observed my brothers chopping it when they would allow me to go with them into the woods years before.

We didn't have much in the way of toys. In fact, we didn't usually receive any toys until Christmastime. Mum always had something for each of us under the tree. Usually we found the Christmas stash early, because she would go shopping early and hide her purchases on the top shelf of the closet, behind some other things. We knew just where to look. Mum had a way of taking minimal resources and turning them into just what we wanted. It wasn't much, but we really appreciated her for doing that, because times were hard and she had little to spend.

On the morning of Christmas, we would wake up early and run into the living room, where the tree stood, and see all the toys and presents. We were not allowed to tear into any presents until our traditional Christmas ceremony was carried out.

That is, we had to read from the Bible, aloud, about the birth of Christ and the true meaning of the Christmas celebration. I wish this tradition could be carried out in families and homes today because of the bond of the holiday with family traditions. When I got married and had kids of my own, I continued this tradition with my family. We would have the kids read aloud Mark's and Matthew's versions of the Virgin birth. After all, this is the true meaning of why we celebrate Christmas.

My daughter, Mona, surprised me this Christmas (2008) when she called on Floyd, my husband, to continue this tradition by reading from the Bible the story of the birth of Jesus. I think our children try very hard not to become as we are in our beliefs and behaviors, but thank God some things are inevitable!

# A Time to Be Happy and a Time to Be Sad

Sadly, everything in our home life was not always happy and fun. There were a few hard and sad occasions in our lives. We tried to focus more on the positives than the negatives and move on. I remember there was this one time that Homer, my stepfather, found a job in Memphis to help supplement the family's lack of income. He worked along with my uncle for a large grocery store there. He would come home on weekends, more times than not, in a drunken state. Mum insisted Homer bring home some portion of the money that he earned. They opened a bank account in both names. She was able to save a nice portion for Christmas. One day she went to the bank to draw out funds for that purpose, and she was told that instead of the six hundred dollars that she thought she had, there was a balance of only sixty dollars! Needless to say, she was devastated, hurt, and angry.

*Forgiveness is always the key to healing and moving on!*

Mum could not wait to confront Homer about the money. She already knew that he had used the money to pay off his liquor bills at several stores in town. She had opened a statement from White's Liquor Store that was addressed to Homer. She must have had that sickly feeling in the pit of her stomach as she read the statement that proved how the money that had been theirs was at a near zero balance according to what he had paid out to White's store.

Another similar situation was when two men in a truck came to our house to take away two of our milking cows, because Homer had used the cows as collateral to pay off his liquor tabs. How could any man owe that much for liquor? We knew the men had taken advantage of Homer, because he paid no attention to what he was signing. I would hear my mum arguing with the men that the cattle did not belong to Homer. And he had no right to sign them over as collateral to Mr. White. Mum had inherited the cows from my father after his death. I think that after a strong argument with the cattle "rustlers," they allowed her to keep the calf, but they took the cow.

Homer would again face the music with Mum as she demanded an explanation of his behavior, again. There was no reasoning with him. He didn't seem to have a clue in his drunken state. He was a good man in many ways, but he was tearing down everything that my mum was working hard to build.

Bud lived with us. He was like a grandfather to us. We loved him. He was generous and compassionate. He was invited to stay on with our family after my father passed away. They had been roommates before my mum and father got married.

Bud received a small welfare check each month to help him with his needs. He would always share a small portion with us in the form of spending change. How is it that he was expected to live on a meager eighty dollars a month? Because Mum was a Good Samaritan, Bud was blessed, and we were blessed to have him there with us. Sometimes he interceded for us when we were about to get our behinds whipped.

One fall evening, when we were home having our traditional Saturday chili supper always provided for by Bud, Homer came home drunk. An argument broke out between the two men. My mum insisted they take the argument outside and remove themselves from our presence. This was a disagreement we had never witnessed before or since.

I think Homer was jealous that Bud gave a lot of attention to us kids and that we loved him as our blood grandfather. Not that this took anything away from Homer. We appreciated him for coming into our lives when our mum had seven children to raise after our father died. Many men would have shied away. My brothers sometimes gave him a hard time, but boys do that in order to put up a bluff to appear tougher than they really are. Homer often brought special treats to my mum, and he gave me a beanie made of felt with different bottle caps punched into the material and sprinkled all over the beanie. It was so unique. I wish I had saved it until this day.

However, the heated argument escalated, and before we knew it, an axe was in the hands of Homer. This action was way more than I had ever seen as a little girl.

My mum gave my sister Louise the shotgun that was once my daddy's, to take over to the Tally's home for safekeeping. She did not want either of the men to get their hands on the gun for fear that, in the heat of the moment, the gun would be used.

When everything was settled, life went on. When she thought they had become more responsible, Mum allowed my brothers to use the gun to go rabbit hunting. This one day in particular, Roland, a family friend, stopped by the house and went with my brothers on the hunting trip. My sister Louise was sick, and she had not been eating properly. Mum decided that maybe she would enjoy her favorite dish of rabbit, rice, and gravy.

Well, at the end of the hunting trip, an accident happened. Our good neighbors and friends, the Saxtons, down the lane from us, had two younger sons who were curious that my brothers had a shotgun walking past their house. As the boys saw my brothers approach them, Roland, who was older than my brothers and had accompanied them on the hunting trip, advised them to break down the gun and make sure the shell was removed from the chamber of the gun and to put on the safety switch.

Evidently they were not fast enough. The older of the two young boys ran around in back of the kneeling boys and swiftly pulled the trigger on the gun, sending the shell into the body of his brother, "Boogie."

That was a very long and sad day for everyone. How could we go on? We were to learn how time heals many wounds. Not that we'll ever stop remembering or filling the void of the loss of a life.

The sheriff was summoned to the scene. The coroner came for the body. A dark shadow fell on the balance of the day and for months to come. We could not go out of the house. My parents went to the Saxton home to give comfort and ask forgiveness for our brother's part in this terrible fatality.

This was the first time that I remember hearing the use of the word "funeral." After the funeral, I don't remember any conversation about the accident. Lives were changed forever. The Winchester gun was put away, never to be used again!

# Home Work Ethics

The greatest manual work anyone could do, as far as I was concerned, was that of picking cotton, especially if you are a child. It was either too hot in August, when we usually began or very freezing cold in November or December, when we were finishing up. My hands would become all scratched and rough from constantly picking the cotton bolls. After a life of this type of work, I never could get my hands ladylike nice and soft as they should be; the results shows even until this day. My facial skin would become very dark and dry from all the exposure to the sun and other elements, especially when the landowner would schedule crop dustings without notice to us. The airplanes would dust the crops with pesticides to kill off the boll weevils that would destroy the young cotton bolls. In the summer, the planes would dust to defoliate the leaves of the cotton plant so the sun could get to the cotton bolls and cause them to open more quickly and fuller.

I tried to dress in layers to protect my skin. One day I had on a hat, gloves, and a long-sleeved shirt. When the boss came out to check on the work's progress, she looked at me and asked my mum if I was a little boy. I didn't like her from that day forward. My brothers laughed and teased me about it.

I dreaded having to do this work, but I knew that there was no other way out of it at the time. It would be my decision to leave, as everyone else did, when I became of age.

Wages that were paid to us for picking cotton by the day amounted to only $2.00. We received a raise to $2.50; later, it was up to $3.00, and when I finally left home for college, wages were a hefty $3.50. We could only pick cotton when we had our fieldwork at home caught up.

When I left for college, I felt guilty at the thought of leaving my mum home to carry on all this work without her children, but I knew I had to do it. It was inevitable. I had to follow my destiny!

Rain became our savior, in that it was about the only thing that would give us relief momentarily from fieldwork. We would rejoice when it would rain. I don't know why, because Mum had a plan for us at home. We would go to the house and begin pumping water for washing clothes, or we would clean the house, for as we knew, "An idle mind is the devil's workshop." My mum had a strong work ethic. She would not be an irresponsible parent, allowing her children to become lazy or spoiled. These words could not exist in our home. This was considered good parenting in olden days.

I was the weakest link when it came to pulling my weight working in the fields. One day—I distinctly remember as if it happened yesterday—I took the liberty of taking an unauthorized break, as I had done many times before. No one could see me lying on my half-filled cotton sack because of the thick foliage on the cotton stalks. Looking up at the bright blue sunny sky and communicating to the heavens, I lamented, "God, if you are up there, please get me outta' here." Needless to say, he had a perfect time and plan for me. I didn't know it, but my destiny was already written. All I needed to do was to be still and allow Him to be God.

When we had picked enough cotton to fill up a wagon, the cotton would be taken to the cotton gin in town to be processed and baled for sale to the highest bidder. Usually, my brothers or stepfather would have that task.

We used to love to play in the cotton. We had a little house out back of our home where we stored the overflow of cotton when the wagon was unavailable or already filled to capacity. Our brothers, the pranksters, would grab us and hold our heads under the cotton as if to smother us. Many times, I thought I would die from suffocation! Our panicky hollering seemed to edge them on even more. How could they understand that we could die? This was their sick way of playing with us.

Those brothers of ours, Jesse and Robert, would also take the cats and pin them by their tails onto the clotheslines when Mum had gone into town to run some errands. They loved to see the cats claw and fight each other when they were pinned too close together on the lines. You've never heard such gnashing and screaming from cats! This behavior was cruel and should not have been done. We actually had too many cats sometimes. Mostly strays. Mum had the boys put about four or five cats into a sack and take them off quite a distance from our house so the cats would find a new home with other families; at least that was her thinking. When my brothers returned home, the cats would be underneath a piece of furniture, peeking out at them as if to ridicule them for their efforts. We were all amazed and laughed our heads off. If that didn't make my day! Well, another day the cats were taken to the river. My brothers were going to make sure the cats didn't return back home; they threw the sack of cats into the river, even as a kid I never condoned this type of behavior, but before the week was gone, the cats had returned again. But the boys would not be outdone!

They never told us the third time what happened to the cats, but we never saw them again. We can only speculate what had happened.

To further emphasize the dysfunctional behavior of my brother Jesse, he would tell my sister and me that he could make a rabbit appear under his hat. We would have to leave the room, and when we returned, there would be a rabbit under his hat. If this did not happen, we could take the wire hanger and beat him with it as hard and as long as the day. Woe! How great was this?

When we returned to the room, we anxiously looked under the hat, believing him and half knowing that no rabbit would be there, but what a great opportunity to take him up on his own word to beat him. It would really fit what we needed to do to get even with him for all of the times that he antagonized us during our short years on this earth. How be it, once again, fowl! No rabbit. Eagerly, I grabbed the wire hanger to have my first wielding blow to his bod; the hanger is as hot as the coals of fire in the stove burn red with intensity. My brother had stuck the end of the wire hanger in the woodstove and handed that end of the hanger to me, searing the skin inside my hand as I grabbed for it.

That branding of my hand was well seared, and the scarring remained until I became an adult (neo-sadist). I love my brother, and this was his sick way of having fun as most boys do! He could have damaged my sister and me for life, physically or mentally. It was good we didn't harbor ill feelings against him.

Hanging with Robert (Bill), Jesse, and their friend Sonny was an occasional pastime. I would climb trees with them, watch them shoot marbles, build birdhouses, and do all those things that were not appropriate for girls to do for fear of being called a tomboy. I didn't care if I was called that it was fun hanging with them. Sometimes they tried to shoo me away, but I persisted and they would let me stay.

Because I was the youngest of seven children, I had fewer chores to do around the house. Children were not exempt from helping the family carry the burden of eking out a living. There were truck patches and gardens to be raised, without a dull moment, ever. My stepfather would plow and cultivate the soil for seasonal plantings; he also planted the melon crops. Our part would be to plant the seedlings of cabbage, tomatoes, potato spuds, and sweet potatoes slips. Usually, Mum would seed the patch of greens, peas, lettuce, cucumbers, beets, radishes, squash, onions, okra, lima beans, carrots, and every other seed known to man. She'd then make sure the garden was weeded until the time of harvest.

"Whiteface", Our dog.

Our table would be a bountiful sight during mealtime. Even the dogs had it good with all the leftovers. Whiteface, our older dog, seemed to know when mealtimes came. He would sit at the back door and wait for us to throw him some bread or table scraps, and he'd catch every morsel thrown to him. We loved feeding him, mainly to watch him catch his food in midair without fail.

As I look back, I know now that the soil on our property richly yielded more than the average harvest! When you calculate the cost of a five-cent package of seed multiplied by all the vegetables on our table every season, the increase would be priceless. Not everyone seemed to know how to be resourceful. There was plenty of land for use if people wanted to put the effort into growing their own produce.

We harvested watermelons by the wagonloads. It was a little difficult bringing the melons from the patch and across a little stream by wagon. We were sure to get stuck. The mules seemed to understand that we had to get the melons across the stream, and they gave it all they had. I'm sure that the reins spurred by a slap against their hides helped. I felt sorry for the mules having to take the whip and pull the heavy load at the same time. We would lose a few melons that rolled off the tipped wagon as it struggled to cross the shallow ravine.

Our watermelon patch was located a distance from the house. We would go out to the melon patch in summertime when the melons were beginning to ripen, and would burst a few open with our fists until we found the sweetest, ripe ones. We were scolded many times for destroying the melons in the field like we did. It was a waste when we didn't wait for the melons to ripen on the vines in the proper time.

Mum would pickle some of the melons, but they never became a popular item with the family. Most of the melons would be taken into town to sell as many as we could.

To set up for the hot and arduous job of canning, we kids had to prepare the jars by cleaning and washing them. We always recycled the Mason jars from one year to the other and purchased new lids so that they would have an airtight seal. Mum would then scald, boil, and sterilize the jars for canning. She treated her work as though it would be judged at the county fair. We often added to her usual list of foods to can by going berry picking. We would bring back gallons of black- and dewberries for her to can. First, she would bake a juicy, buttery blackberry cobbler for dinner. Mum had an awesome sweet tooth, which translated to many delectable desserts at mealtime.

My personal chore was to churn the milk once or twice a week. I was about nine years old when I inherited this chore. Churning milk would produce rich butter, and the resulting buttermilk was good for drinking and baking. I didn't like milk. Even today, it is hard for me to drink a glass of milk without remembering the harsh smell of curdled milk. We had gallons of milk available to us, and it was consumed by us straight from the cow, no pasteurization! My stepfather would milk the cows. The unconsumed gallons of milk would be set aside for the milk to curdle and churn, usually the next day. Churning milk by hand using a dasher and churn caused much splashing and sloshing just to get the job done.

Mum would pour the creamy pliable butter into a wooden mold and allow it to firm in the refrigerator. When it was removed from the mold the next morning, it would look as thought it was purchased at the store.

My brothers and older sister, Louise, knew how to milk the cows, too. I could never get the hang of it. They would have me open my mouth, and they'd squirt milk directly into my mouth from the cow's teat. The milk would be warm and different from the taste of homogenized, refrigerated milk.

I don't know exactly where or when, but we acquired a goat. He had a pen all to himself. We would not go near him, because he used his head to butt things, and people, too, if he was given the chance. Now, goat's milk we did not like or want, and we were told that the meat of the animal was a little musty, like venison. We decided he would not be a keeper, especially since he would somehow reach his head over the fence and pull Mum's clean clothes from the line and chew them up. I was thoroughly flabbergasted when he chewed up my new cowboy suit that my cousin Clarence, from Memphis, had let me have. To this day, I will not eat goat cheese, or goat anything for that matter.

As I grew older, and since I was the last child living at home, I would come home from school at least once a month to find a note from Mum to make cornbread to go with the beans or greens that she left cooking on the stove. There was no recipe for me to follow. No one had taught me how to make cornbread, so my first experience with cooking or baking anything was for me to recall the ingredients and the process from being in the kitchen when Mum cooked.

My first attempt was okay. The bread was too thick but decent for the first time. I was hooked. Now that I had passed the test, other cooking responsibilities were thrown in. Never show that you know how to do a thing well, because you'll be stuck with doing that chore all the time. The good thing was I was never required to cook an entire meal.

Sometime later, my next dish I was told to bake was an apple pie, and after I had completed that task, I had permission to attend the water carnival that was held at White River in DeValls Bluff each year on Labor Day. It was always a great event. There would be speed-boating, acrobats on water skis, cotton candy, food vendors—all with a big carnival atmosphere. It was so much fun. This event kicked off the beginning of school and cotton-picking season. To school the blessed would go, and to the fields the rest would go!

When I was eleven years old, I began working for Mrs. Summers. She owned a store, and the back space was her residence. I started out just washing dishes for her. Later, I would work for her on Saturdays and some days after school. During the summer months, I could work an entire week when cotton-harvesting time was over. She would pay me around $15.00 a week. Sometimes I would share some of my earnings with my mum.

Working for Mrs. Summers allowed me to purchase most of my school clothing and accessories. I bought my first watch at Betzner's Store with some of my earnings. It was a Timex with a pink leather band that cost $6.95. That watch lasted from age thirteen until I was in college. I was one of the best-dressed kids at school. My principal even complimented me once on how well my appearance was at school. He said that I never *follow* trends; I *set* them. After I learned to sew, I would purchase material from Mrs. Summers's store and make my own fashions. I could buy almost anything I wanted at the store, because I would have the opportunity to purchase items on credit and "work it off" from week to week.

Mrs. Summers had been a good influence on me learning some things about cooking as well. She would have me help her cut up the veggies for soup or combine ingredients for making chicken and dumplings, shell lima beans, or do other food prep duties. I watched her cook and learned how to season different foods.

In high school, I was invited by Ms. Odom to work in the school cafeteria along with other students Mildred Saxton and Duck Wright. We would help prep for lunch and set up serving trays and utensils for the lunch students.

Earseline, our head cook, had excellent culinary skills. In exchange for our help in the cafeteria, we were allowed to eat our lunch free; lunches were only fifteen cents. From the experience, we received more than a free lunch; we received other duties concerning cafeteria training. We could even have breakfast if we prepared it!

No matter that we had the awesome responsibility to get up at five o'clock each morning and return home at six o'clock in the evening during cotton-planting and harvesting season, to work all day long in the hot, dry, and arid fields, an unending list of other chores always awaited us, such as, pumping water for cooking, cleaning, washing, and bathing and watering the pigs, cows, horses, and chickens. (Chores unending!)

Laundry took most of a day to complete. Each load of clothes needed to boil in an outdoor water-filled kettle. Mum made her own soap. Those white sheets would be whiter than white, with the fresh smell of a dew-sprinkled morning, when we'd take them in after they dried. Everything had to be hung so-so on the clothing lines. All whites together, light coloreds, and then dark clothing. Jessie Sanders would have it no other way.

Mum bought her chicks through mail order. They usually arrived at the post office in the springtime. She would have us stop by the post office after school to see if her order of Rhode Island Reds, Bantams, and White Leghorns had come in. We needn't ask the postmaster, because the loud, "cheep, cheep, cheep" could be heard as soon as we entered the post office. The tiny, fluffy-feathered baby chicks would be there, waiting for someone to pick them up. They arrived in a large square box with cutout circles and enough water and feed to tide them over until Homer could drive the tractor or horses into town to retrieve our future chicken dinners and the many dozen eggs they would provide.

When these little babies transformed into adult chickens, we would take turns collecting eggs from the laying hens in the chicken house. Sometimes, there would be about a dozen eggs per day. Mum would give away eggs, milk, and food items, because there would be much too much for us to consume ourselves.

Selling eggs, pecans, and butter was often a source of income so we could purchase other staples that were needed from the store, such as, flour, sugar, salt, seasonings, and the like. There were no frills in our household.

You would think that since the cost of bread was something like fifteen cents, pop was five cents, and a slice of baloney, cheese, and crackers all were five cents for the lot, that we'd have more. The thing was, the cost of living was low, but wages were way, way low. I have this information on good authority, because as kids, we would order such things when we went into town on Saturday evenings for our weekly recreation. Mike, Corine, Stine, Barbara Ann, and sometimes Nona Marie, along with yours truly, headed straight to Betzners' store to get our Saturday evening special, which came with a Barqs orange, strawberry, or grape pop. Actually, Nehi was my favorite brand. In our part of the South, we called it soda water; in Gary, it was just soda; and in Chicago, they called it pop. Anyway, we would walk around town, eating and waiting for dark to come so we could go sneaking into the movies without parental approval. We knew that if we asked, the answer would be a flat-out no.

By the time we walked in one direction, which was about two blocks in length east to west, and the same area from north to south, we had finished our snacks.

We would alternate Saturdays eating in the streets and going to Annie Thompson's Restaurant. Actually, it was her two-story residence, where she had a restaurant downstairs for the uptown visitors. My favorite supper at her place would be the chili. She made the best! A bowl of chili with crackers would cost only ten cents, add a soda water, and you'd have a dime left of your allotment of twenty-five cents.

This little ritual in town on Saturdays had to slow down when I took on my first job working for Mrs. Summers.

I missed running with the gang so much on Saturdays, but making my own money working for Mrs. Summers was too good to miss!

Once I went with my cousin and best bud, Lola, to Frank Hendricks Café, where music was always playing on the jukebox, and Lola loved to dance. I was so afraid I would get caught, or that someone would tell my mum that I was at this off-limits café; that would be curtains for me. During this time, we were in high school.

# Recreation and Community Relations

Mum loved going fishing with Cousin Ola. The lake was within walking distance from our house. You know, my sister and I had to go along with them, because we were too small to be left alone at home. They would make a day of it, bringing the deep-frying iron skillet, lard, and whatever else would be needed to clean and fry the fish on the spot. The fish frys were such a drag for me. Mum and Cousin Ola would try to keep me amused by cutting a young sapling for a fishing pole. I would cast its line into the lake but to no avail. Nothing ever happened for me! Amazingly, they caught enough for a meal and then some. We would eat fish along with other foods they packed for the outing.

It was interesting the way that the ladies in Mum's circle of friends would go from house to house during the winter months after the fields were harvested. They would take turns hosting the quilting bee. The quilting frames would be brought out, and the ladies would gather around the setup, laughing, talking, eating, and quilting all day long.

I looked forward to when it was Mum's turn, because we knew some special leftover goodies would be ours after we returned home from school at the end of the day. I'm not talking chips and dips, but southern fried chicken, potato salad, and cobbler or cake from the soul food chain. Additionally, we would have a new, beautiful quilt added to our collection.

The ladies of the quilting bee would exchange patterns for making the quilts. My favorite quilt patterns were the double wedding rings, the wagon wheel, and the great starburst! They were so colorful and creative. Of the appliqués, my favorite was the little Dutch girl. When I was older, I made a quilt using the butterfly appliqué patterned after Mum's little Dutch girl. I considered it beautiful, and I made all by myself!

The Bible study group would meet on alternate weeks at different homes for fellowship and to study the word of God. The house would be filled with the warmth of friendship and shared foods.

I joined the 4-H club at the age of twelve, and my friend Mildred's mother, Angeline, would take us all to the annual competition at the county fairgrounds. Angeline always encouraged us to enter in one category or another. My entry would be something that I had made in home economics, such as an apron, a pillowcase, or a skirt. We had also learned to crochet at the time, but I never entered anything that I had done.

One year, Mum won a ribbon for her canned peaches. We also had sewn aprons in home economics class at school, and it became an entry as well. Honorable mention was about all we received! The experience and fun we had going to the fair was well worth it all.

The National Homemakers of America Club (NHA) helped to prepare us for leadership roles through presentations and training we received in home economics. Mrs. Lusk, our instructor, was an excellent teacher, who gave us the necessary resources that would benefit us for a lifetime.

In our home economics building, we had nice, new, lounge furniture, a modern kitchen, and classroom facilities. We had classes such as, "On Becoming a Young Lady," "Do's and Don'ts," "Physiological Changes in the Female Body," and "Proper Etiquette," as well as ones about preparing and cooking breakfast and properly setting a table. I worked in the group with Carolyn, because she already knew these things. Her dad was a chef. We even planned a tea party for a Sunday afternoon and invited others to participate. It was to show that we had learned good social graces.

I wasn't acquainted with voting as a youngster, but my parents would go to the polls at every opportunity, because they did not always have that privilege years ago.

Bud was about thirty years older than my mum, and he would tell us stories of how his parents were ex-slaves and some of the abuse they suffered as slaves. He was honored to live as a free man. He said that in order for his generation to vote, blacks had to pass a literacy test that was given at the polls. Some examples of the questions on the test were: "How many bubbles are in a bar of soap?" "How many jelly beans in a jar?" and "How many breaths does a person take in a day?" Did they vote? No! Could these people who designed the test pass it themselves? No. How absurd!

It was much later that some of the inequities related to freed slaves were gradually abolished. We were still second-class citizens living under the residuals of the old masters.

When I was in high school and after I was in college, Mum would take me to the polls with her. I think she needed someone just to stand with her, as there seemed to always be an air of intimidation surrounding the polling stations. I even remember that hostile atmosphere as a youngster. Whites worked and ran the precincts and polling places. They would stare you down when you came to the place to vote and you were black. It was as though you weren't supposed to be there.

# Segregation vs. Integration

As a child, I was uninformed as to the real meaning of segregation. I thought this was just how the world was: whites living separate, attending their own church, restaurants, schools, and achieving most of the benefits from the economic pie.

I cannot remember exactly when I learned that the *separation* of the races meant that we were *segregated*. It had been such an acceptable evil for so many years that no one questioned it. We all had become too comfortable with it!

When I was a small child, my surrogate grandfather, whom we called "Bud," would sometimes take us on the bus to visit his daughter, who lived in Brinkley. As we waited for the bus one day, we decided to get a cool drink of water from a fountain on the side of the building at the bus depot. We saw the sign over the fountain that read, "Whites only."

On our way home on the bus, we found seats up front behind the driver to be the best choice for us, because we would be able to see out of the large windows. When the driver saw us sitting there, he yelled, "You niggers get to the back of the bus." We obliged. I overheard my grandfather apologize to the driver as he got on the bus behind us, telling the driver that we were just kids and didn't know any better. We removed our happy little selves to the back of the bus.

In town was a café where we loved to go and get a sour pickle and occasionally a hamburger and soda when we had the funds. At the café, blacks had to enter through the back door, and whites could enter through the front door. A similar case was at the movie theater; blacks would sit at the second level of the theater and had no access to the concession stands. The smell of popcorn drove us crazy! However, the opportunity to view movies such as *Roy Rogers, Flash Gordon, Buster Crabbe The Cisco Kid, The Lone Ranger, My Friend Flicka, Lassie,* and others turned out to be forgiving enough for us.

White kids attended school in DeValls Bluff, and black kids attended school in Biscoe. I often wondered why, in every book that was assigned to me, there were lists of other students' names that I did not recognize. I would read through the names and discover that these students did not attend our school. They had to have been students from DeValls Bluff's campus. This also meant that our school received their recycled books, while they got all the new books.

When I was in high school, I observed that our typewriters were old, mostly inoperable, and needed to be thrown away. I loved typing class and was good at it. The realization was that the white schools had gotten new typewriters, and the old ones were sent over to our school. We had to struggle with the machinery, but we had to make it work.

During the summer after the end of eleventh grade, I went to Memphis to visit my aunt Essie and her family. During my stay there, I met a young man who was a friend of my cousin Clarence. Exum invited me to attend a sit-in that had been planned by college youth. Since I was a senior in high school, I felt honored to be asked to participate.

The target stores were the Five and Dime and Woolworth lunch counters, where blacks were not allowed service. I was so excited to be a part of this change for the black population of the city, but as my aunt explained, I would have to call her if the police arrested us and took us to jail, and the responsibility would be on her to bail me out.

I thought long and hard about it and decided that this would not be fair to her. So, for this historical event, I needed to step back. I had this great passion to help my race achieve on the battleground of desegregation. The results of these sit-ins were that the drugstore soda fountains and lunch counters were removed from stores.

In 1957, at the age of fifteen, my sister self-emancipated herself, married Jim (with Mum's permission), moved to New York, and then moved to Little Rock, Arkansas. Central High School was just a few blocks down the street from where she and her husband lived. When I visited them, I watched the high school kids walk past her home. Among those students was Elizabeth Eckford, one of the Little Rock Nine, a title given to the nine students who integrated Central High School in 1957. Elizabeth and my sister, Stine, became casual friends and would sometimes chat as she passed her home. Stine and Elizabeth were the same age.

The whole world was watching the daily turn of events that led to desegregation in our schools. Every evening we would sit around the TV with family members to watch the famous Nine take the taunts, verbal abuse, and name-calling of whites who would gather there daily for that expressed purpose. They had a chant that they used to taunt the Nine further. They repeated it over and over: "2-4-6-8, we don't want to integrate!" One of the nine just got tired of it all and retaliated by spitting on one of the hecklers. Sadly, she was expelled for a week.

The governor of Arkansas at that time was Orval E. Faubus. His most infamous words, as spoken on TV news were, "I will not force my people to integrate."

Not long after those infamous words by our governor, we all fell in love with President Dwight D. Eisenhower, all over again. In 1958, on a special TV broadcast, he declared that the 101st Division Infantry Division would be deployed to Little Rock Central High School to ensure that each of the nine students would be personally escorted to school after Governor Faubus prevented the nine from entering school on the first day. History was being made right before our eyes! I would imagine that shouts of joy coming from every black household for at least a mile away, listening to TV while as President Dwight Eisenhower stepped in to step up!

In Little Rock, Daisy Bates was involved with the NAACP and other organizations that supported justice for blacks at a time when our nation seemed to believe that justice under the law was for whites only! Bates was a friend and advocate for the Little Rock Nine.

Levels of consciousness were being raised throughout the South concerning desegregation. There were a lot of unsettled minds and angry dissidents in the South.

Signs of bigotry slowly began to come down. Seating arrangements on public transportation were no longer assigned black and white. Slowly, schools began to integrate according to a court-ordered decree.

My friend Mildred invited me to attend a town hall meeting where attorney John Walker answered questions and informed citizens of the black community of their rights under the Constitution of the United States of America. Whites were meeting in secret places to determine what would and could be done; they were not about to send their kids to school with blacks! This was not going to be easy. A fight was brewing!

*Life Is a Story*

*The Civil Rights Act of 1965 was only written on paper at this time …*

*The struggle continued.*

I worked at a motel in DeValls Bluff to earn some cash for college the summer of the hot early '60s. One day while I was in the restaurant's kitchen helping out, the TV monitor was visible to us from the dining area. Each evening, everyone intensely watched news updates on the situation at Central High School.

On one particular evening, a teacher from DeValls Bluff High School came into the restaurant to have dinner. As he entered the dining area, we could hear his derogatory comments about the nine students, saying, "They have those niggers on the news again?" Well, the kitchen help was sick of his daily comments and had a surprise in store for him. Once he came in late when all the food had been thrown away for the day because it was so near closing time. The retaliatory crew retrieved all the food he needed from the garbage and neatly arranged it on his plate!

At a time during the early '60s when Dr. King was making us aware of the injustices of our society, an energetic young attorney named John Walker began filing legal appeals in the court in Little Rock. It has been four decades and four years since President Lyndon B. Johnson signed the Civil Rights Act of 1964 into law. African Americans know that laws in small southern towns are still hard-nosed. It had been hard to right the wrongs enacted by the injustices of over two hundred years.

In 1966, I became the first black teacher to integrate the all-white DeValls Bluff school system. I was not given a teaching position but an assignment as the elementary school librarian. It was a "token" position, an appeasement for integration if you will! I was willing to be the patsy, however, desegregation was inevitable. With this assignment,

I received training at State College of Arkansas, at the expense of the school district, to prepare myself for the librarian position.

On my first day's assignment at the all-white elementary school, a little boy ran through the hallway yelling to everyone after he had seen me enter the building, "Hey everybody, we've got a nigger teacher." The following year, one more teacher was added, and more blacks were slowly phased in as mandated by the court's ruling. I never felt intimidated or angry at individuals, but I was disappointed at the system.

In 1969, we moved to Gary, Indiana, where Mayor Richard Gordan Hatcher had been elected as the first black mayor in the city's history. I wanted to be there! Things in the South were moving too slowly. The resistance to change was overwhelming. Again history has recorded a blight against justice and a spot on the pages of our Constitution.

# Morals and Values

Church and home teachings gave us our sense of values and lifelong morals. Without exception, we had to attend church every Sunday morning and late into the evening. Sometimes we returned home at one or two o'clock the next morning. Additionally, we would have Tuesday evening prayer service as well as Saturday evening young people's service. Church was very demanding, and our conduct was to be in line with our beliefs and principles.

My first pastor and his wife, Elder and Mrs. W. J. Johnson.

There are fond memories of our pastor, Elder W. J. Johnson, and his family, who came from North Little Rock each weekend, very faithfully, to serve as church pastor. He would pick up and drive all members who had no transportation to church. Most members lived in close proximity to the church and could walk.

Elder Johnson was successful in establishing a youth ministry and would put in hours of time with us not only in church but take us to out-of-town meetings to elevate our spiritual and moral growth.

Elder Johnson was like a son for my mum and, therefore, a big brother to all of us. Mum seemed to really love church and its members. It was her life. When Elder Johnson came to Biscoe to become the pastor of our small, rundown church, his goal was to rebuild the church.

How could our pastor come into this small farming town and ask its small, poor membership to contribute money to build a new church? He had an infectious faith in God and the spiritual ability to do the work of the Lord.

When Elder Johnson laid out the plan to rebuild for the members, I observed the reaction of the members, who were mostly women. (We only had about four male members.) Heads began turning, faces were frowning, and the quiet chatter among the members didn't seem too optimistic. Our church members were made up mainly of widows, sharecroppers, and seniors on welfare. Elder Johnson had asked each member to pledge one hundred dollars for the first year. One hundred dollars could have been the same as one thousand in the day! It was money we did not have.

To raise their portions of the pledge, Mum and her friends immediately got busy selling fish or chicken dinners on Saturdays and ice cream and pound cake for dessert from Mrs. Evelyn's house. They seemed excited and, by faith, motivated to do the work of the Lord! Fund-raisers continued corporately as well as individually.

Elder Johnson didn't just ask the membership for pledges, he was the model for giving himself. He gave far above anything that he had asked of his members. He was the perfect example!

Before we knew it, we had a down payment toward our new building. Praise God! Another two years or so, and we had a new edifice that the community could be proud of. A friend of Elder Johnson, Elder Quick, was the contracted builder. The building has been improved on over the years.

My last visit through the city, in 2006, found our church still standing as one of the nicest buildings in the town. It is still amazing how a few members with nonexistent jobs worked diligently to help build the church. It proves again that if you are willing and have purpose in your heart to do a thing, you can achieve your goal.

When we went to church on Saturday evening, sometimes we would sneak away to the movies or visit the stores and purchase a slice of cheese, lunch meats, pop, and crackers. We would walk around town with Mike, Corine, Barbara Ann, and at other times, Nona, Lolarene, and Flo Catherine. We loved these junk-food items, because at our house, Mum never purchased them for us since we had an abundance of natural foods that were always available to us. We often got into trouble by sneaking off to the movies. We viewed the movie from the second level of the theater; whites watched the movie from the first floor.

We were not allowed to go to school socials, dances, sports games, movies, and other such sinful events. Not so much that these things are sinful, but that the Bible says to, "be careful to be seated in the midst of sinners," which was the way it was explained to us.

Our pastor blended some parts of our youth services with the main church services. We were encouraged to take part in testimony services,

YPWW (Young People's Willing Workers), and Sunday school so that we didn't feel left out.

Mum was a very religious woman. Her life was an example and model for us to follow. Not all of us would choose her way. She had decided to live her life for Christ and to take us kids, hollering and screaming along the way. Out of all this, we accepted the call.

When Mum said a thing, it was law. We would not argue, question, or go against anything she did or said, at least not openly. We may have had some thoughts of our own, but we respected her as well as all adults in a like manner. That is how we were taught.

I'm not saying that this adoption of Mum's beliefs made us kids perfect. We all fall down, but the important thing is that we get up again!

At the time, I didn't really know or had not come into the revelation concerning God's perfect grace and his unconditional love for us all. For me, it all became engrained and entwined into my life, even as an adult.

After all my teachings, I should confess that I took three pennies from Mrs. Gray's desk when I was a first-grade student in her class. During recess, she would sell those little peanut butter logs for three cents each. Seems everyone except me had three cents to purchase a candy. I wanted one too, and I saw the pennies on her desk and made myself welcome to them. I bought the candy, but somehow I couldn't enjoy it for the guilty feelings I had.

After recess was over, Mrs. Gray asked who took the three pennies from her desk. Did she really think someone would come forth and confess? She claimed that she knew who had taken the money. Somehow I didn't believe her. I'm sure she was trying to bring the guilty person forward. She seemed to be leaning toward one of the suspect boys. I sure felt the compulsion to confess. You would have thought that someone had taken three or thirty dollars.

I would make it up to her one day, I decided. But somehow I never did, except I tried to be the very best student that I possibly could, and maybe one day she would be proud of me and forgive me for the indiscretion I had committed.

Mrs. Elma Gray was one of the best teachers I knew. She helped hundreds of students learn to read, write, and do arithmetic. She was very kind to me and all of her students. I wished that I had not betrayed her trust by taking the pennies, but it was done.

Another one of my deceptive behaviors was the time my sister Stine and I were pulling our dolls in our brothers' little, red, Radio Flyer wagon. It had rained outside, and a little fluke of an accident happened. The wagon tipped over, and my doll fell out of the rear end of the wagon into a mud puddle of water. At that time, dolls were made of a very porous material, and the face of my dolly puckered, peeled, and slid off; the rest of her body was completely ruined! We had just gotten those dolls for Christmas, and now mine was ruined.

Well, one day we were in town and paid a visit to my cousin Birdie Ree's house. She was living with her grandmother at the time. Birdie Ree allowed Stine and me to play with her dolls during our visit. Birdie had several dolls. Stine told her that my doll had fallen into the puddle and had to be thrown away. I hinted to her that I really liked her dolls and would like to have another doll for myself. She said she would speak to her grandmother to see if it would be okay for me to have one of hers. She didn't do it that day. But on another occasion when I was in town, I went over to their house and told Mrs. Hattie, Birdie's grandmother, that Birdie Ree said I could have one of her dolls. Birdie Ree was not at home, so Mrs. Hattie was hesitant about giving me the doll without speaking with her granddaughter about it first. I assured her that Birdie Ree said I could have it, and she brought out two dolls and asked me which one of the dolls Birdie promised me. I chose the doll that was not as pretty as the other one, for obvious reasons, and she let me have it.

This was not the whole truth, but I got away with it. Again, I couldn't be completely happy playing with the doll because I had obtained it under false pretenses. Birdie Ree never questioned me about it, so I decided that I was in the clear.

My mum always thought it was the same doll that I had gotten for Christmas, because they were very similar and I had not told her about the mishap with my dolly. She didn't know to say anything to me about it.

I was not setting a precedent in deceptive like behavior for my life. I knew better. I think I can chalk this up to *childlike* behavior. I never took anything that did not belong to me ever again in my life. I had learned my lesson early on in the way of a convicted conscience.

Farming in a small town did not allow for a lot of socialization. If you were part of a large family, as we were, you were blessed to have your siblings to bounce around and interact with. The downside of this presented a false sense of reality. We had little to measure ourselves against. We had no idea of what ideals the rest of America held. Watching TV began to reveal the best and worst that society had to offer. We needed to filter and choose.

When I was about nine or ten years of age, there was this white man who would come around in the early fall selling aromatic, juicy, large apples in many baskets from the back of his truck. He would invite each of us, one at a time, into the bed of his truck to pick out a free apple for ourselves. What we didn't know was that this guy was taking advantage of us. We were very vulnerable, because our parents were in the fields and we were not acquainted with this type of behavior. When he lifted us into his truck, he would *accidentally* touch us in an inappropriate way. Because we were innocent kids, we didn't realize the sexual implication of his behavior. We never heard of the word "sex" in anyone's vocabulary at that point. It was not until school started the following year that I overheard my cousin telling my sister about this man who had touched her older sister in an inappropriate way, and they were all upset about it. She had threatened to tell her parents after this had occurred more than one time, but he never came around our houses after that. We had not heard the last of him!

One day during recess, we went across the street to the mom and pops candy store, and who would be there but this old apple salesman, who was up to his same old antics. He made his move on one of the students, and a report of his actions got back to the principal. After that, our principal would not allow us to go to the store. This man's behavior was my first experience where an adult took liberties with innocent children. We all knew this was an isolated incident and that we would not let this dim our trust in grown-ups, who should be there to help and protect us. It was scary, but we got past it and put it out of our minds for the time being.

Our parents did not have conversation with us concerning sex and what to do and what not to do if we were approached in an inappropriate way. Schools addressed the issues on a small scale. We all talked and behaved in the way modeled for us by our parents through morals and beliefs that were understood and passed down through generations.

Author Ernestine May from earlier days.

Bud and our mule.

Wylie Leonard.

Buddy, Bud's only son, who lived in Omaha, NE.

Family Day with Mum, Aunt Tressie, Mae, Louise, Billy, and little friend.

*Life Is a Story*

Arthur Meadows, my father, with five of my sisters and brothers.

My niece Margaret Ann.

Homer and Mum at the corner grocery store.

Mum's good friend, Mrs. Evelyn Clark.

My little niece, Joyce, who at 5 years old, was still carrying a bottle around with her.

Mum with my sister Augustine

Mum and Joyce.

Jessie Hall-Meadows-Sanders, "Mum"

Mum with my niece, Pam.

Uncle Frank, Mum, Stine, Joyce, Margaret, and me.

# Early School to College Days

*We can do all things through Christ, who strengthens us!*

We had no kindergarten program in Arkansas, so I entered first grade at the age of six. Our first-grade class was combined with the second grade because of a low school enrollment. Elementary school became a defining time in my life. Mum would give me a quarter each morning for lunch, and I'd have a dime left to spend on whatever. I would buy school supplies such as pencils (one cent each), composition book, crayons, or coloring books (five cents). At this early age of my schooling, I didn't have chores in the fields. Although that would come much too soon! I think my mum wanted to give her last child a jump-start on education.

Mum had an old, pedal-model Singer sewing machine that she used to whip up our flour- and feed-sack clothing. The feed sacks of muslin would be bleached and used mostly for undergarments, while the much colorful, floral, flour sacks were used for skirts and dresses.

Mum made most of Stine's and my dresses for school until we were old enough to realize there were clothing in stores that we desired more. Mum always said it only mattered that our clothing was neat and clean. We were beginning to see through that phrase. We still wanted something a little better.

When I was about seven years old, our insurance man, who came to collect Mum's life insurance premiums, would stop by our house every other week. Mum usually had food cooking on the stove when he arrived. He would head straight toward the kitchen and begin tasting food directly from the pots on the stove (ugh). He would say, "Jessie, my goodness, what are you cooking? I sure wish my wife could cook like this!"

But we forgave him, because he became the bearer of gifts to us in the form of many beautiful dresses that his daughters had outgrown. The clothing was in excellent condition, expensive looking and seemed hardly ever worn.

There were fresh colored plaids, checks, stripes, floral, and solid patterns. We were so blessed by this God-sent gentleman. He was a credit to his company and a generous witness to people helping others.

When Mum passed some forty years later, her insurance policy with the Life of Georgia was still active. We were able to use it to help defray the cost of her funeral.

Prairie County Training School was the school that I attended before the name was changed. First-grade through high school students were housed at this campus site. Lower elementary students were housed in the back building. Middle- and high school students were in the two-story, red brick building at the front grounds. We had a very nice home economics building and a gymnasium. The gym was appropriately named for Ms. Helen A. Odom, the oldest teacher at the high school.

I loved the idea of going to school, and I never thought I would enjoy school as much as I did. I didn't even mind having to run almost every morning because we nearly always missed the bus. Most times, we would take the shortcut across the cemetery to get to the bus stop at Highway 70. The driver would have to pick us up early and drop us off at our all-black school and then pick up the white students in Biscoe to take them to the all-white DeValls Bluff School. (Hence, criss-crossing schools to avoid integration.) Once it was raining very hard, and the run across the cemetery would certainly be no fun. We were happy when Billy Tally, our neighbor, picked us up in his dad's Model T Ford with the back rumble seat. What an experience to ride in that seat! It was also a day my brothers were trying to ride their bikes to school, and the bikes had to be put into the small backseat as well.

Because my birthday is in February, I had to wait until September of the following year before enrolling in school. When my sister and brothers would come home from school each day, Mum required each one of them to read to her. They sat on the floor in front of her and read the pages of their assigned story aloud. I would listen attentively as they read.

Sometimes I would pick up their books after they were finished for the day and try and read for myself. Since my sister Augustine was closer to my age, I learned to read her book first because the words were easier. I was so happy to go to school with my sister, Augustine, and brothers the following September.

My first year in school I read all the pre-primer readers, the primer, and the first-grade reader. I knew how to read front and center. So, my teacher, Mrs. Gray, promoted me to the second-grade reader, which gave me a double promotion my first year in school. I loved that I caught up with my sister in second grade.

I still remember some of the stories that I read, such as *Sandy Wants a Home* and the story of *Benjamin B.* Everyone of my generation should remember *Fun with Dick and Jane*.

I mentioned earlier that education is enlightenment. For example, I was in second grade when I read a story that revealed information to me about people in other parts of the world. In social studies, it was Lars of Lapland. Lars was a little boy who was a sheepherder, possibly in the mountainous countryside of Finland. The accompanying page showed a map to designate the place where he lived. I studied the pictures of Lars and the countryside carefully and wondered about his family life. Yet, we had something in common. Lars lived on a farm, too!

I began to look for evidence of other people in faraway lands. I was intrigued to say the least. From these experiences, I developed an interest in finding out more about people in other countries. I wanted to know more. How is it that their language, customs, dress, and traditions are so different from mine? This interest led me in later life to open my doors to sponsor foreign exchange students from five different countries, linking three continents!

Second grade was the beginning of other spurts of intellectual growth and further dreams and aspirations of being the person I was created to be. I was always the dreamer. Even today, my head is filled with *what has been, what could be, and how can I attain my purpose in life?*

I made a double promotion my first year in school and was so elated that I found an occasion to tell everyone I met on my way home from school. Stine, my sister in second grade, was not pleased that I was in the same class with her.

We usually walked home from school, and as soon as we crossed the tracks to Beatrice Black's café, we stopped in. Sometimes when we had a nickel or a dime we would do this. Get a soda, a cake, or something to eat along the way home. When I told Mrs. Beatrice that I had made second grade in my first year, she gave me a whole soda to congratulate me.

Later, when we came to town with our mum (Beatrice was one of my Mum's good friends), we observed Beatrice pouring the leftover pop from her customers together to refill bottles, which she resold to new customers. We said, "Ugh." I never wanted her pop again.

When Mum would visit her friend Beatrice socially, she allowed us to play in her backyard. Her place of residency was at the back end of the café that she owned, which is what was called a "storefront" home. The neat thing about playing in her backyard was that the newer construction was further toward the back lot of the property, and the newer one was built forward of the old. That meant we had a discovery zone where the old building had been. We found many coins to pocket as a result of the burned-out building. We told Beatrice about the coins we had found, however, she said we could have anything that we found back there. She didn't think that the coins would amount to anything but a few pennies, but even so, they were a treasure to us.

Another adventurous treat was the walk of about three miles after school across the fields to Mum's friend Coot Harris's house. He and his wife had no kids, so they welcomed us to their home to watch the *Mickey Mouse Club*; it was so popular and every kid's favorite show. We didn't have a TV at the time. At the Harris's house, we could also play outside in their yard, and we would find all of the beautiful and colorful marbles, half hidden in he soil, some appearing as cat eyes, others were large aggies. Our brothers loved that, because they liked playing marbles with Sonny and LC Saxton. They were really good at it. I could only watch them from the sidelines. When Sonny or LC was not around, Jesse would let me play marbles with him. Sonny was so good that he entered different marble-shooting competitions, and most of the time he won.

I remember one year my family had worked hard in the fields and realized a small profit at the end of the season. Usually, we just broke even! Mum decided that the boys had worked along with her to help make our year's end a success and purchased bikes for each of them. They were *some* glad. I resolved in my heart that I would learn to ride the bicycle. They were having too, too much fun on those bikes. Ask me to see my effort scars, because I have a few! Jesse and Bill did not want us riding their precious bikes, so I went to play with Sadie Mae. She had a girl's bike that was even easier for me to ride.

On day I stopped by Sadie Mae's house after school and had so much fun riding her bike that I forgot all sense of time and arrived at home much too late. Needless to say, that never happened again!

I loved playing with my friends and getting to spend the night sometimes with my cousin Lolarene, who was also my best friend. Carolyn, another of my friends, invited me to spend the night at her home. Both friends were real cool. Lola was real hip. Carolyn was studious and smart. They taught me a lot about life. One taught me from a social point of view, and the other taught me from an intellectual perspective.

One of those embarrassing moments in my life was when Carolyn came to my house to spend the night with me. I had not gone to school that day because I had to work in the fields. When we returned home, Carolyn was sitting on our porch waiting for me. I said, "Oh, my gosh!" I was very surprised and unprepared. In comparison, Carolyn had everything in a home life, whereas, I had very little. For example, at her house, we had eggs, bacon, and toast for breakfast, and at my house, we had warmed-over spaghetti soup. Although this was not a typical breakfast, even for us, it just happened to be one of those times when we were operating at the lowest level of income. Needless to say, Carolyn passed on breakfast.

To give further insight for comparison, Carol's dad had a legit job and a car. We had two mules and a tractor that belonged to the landowner. These facts didn't seem to matter with Carolyn; she as was a really great person. She was my friend.

As students, we spent many hours preparing for our end-of-the-year school performances. Every elementary class chose a night to perform. The year that I hold dear was the year that I was in the third grade, and we performed with the second-graders. I don't remember the title of the play, but we were chickens, ducks, and other barnyard animals. We were all dressed in the appropriate costumes. I learned everyone's part, including my own. When it was time for my friend Lynn to say his part, he was fast asleep. I gave him a big hunch, as he sat next to me in the makeshift chicken coop. I cued him on the lines to say to keep the play moving. The audience roared!

In an annual tradition, on the first day of May, some of the teachers would plan to erect the Maypole. They would decorate the top of the pole with colorful streamers and teach us how to go in and out of a configuration to braid the pole with flowing, colorful crepe paper. Each teacher made a crown of colorful paper flowers to encircle our heads. Music would be played and songs sang as we danced around the Maypole. The end result was a beautifully braided pole.

We were a small town with a small school population, regardless of the fact that we accommodated students from other towns and communities as well. However, we had other activities that helped us to build character and responsibilities, such as, basketball, volleyball, baseball, choir, school plays, and hayrides in the fall.

For further socialization and competition with other nearby schools, we had a Field Day in the early spring that became a venue for students in oratorical contests, talent shows, intellectual skills, physical, and creative competitions. Biscoe was hard to beat! Who could beat Marcia (Tut) McDonald and LaVonne (Pepper) Holloway at orations? Especially, if coached by our principal, Mr. McBeth, Mrs. Elma Gray, or Mrs. Sarah Stidham! Teachers seemed to have had an exorbitant amount of flowing energy to spend so much time with the students.

Biscoe High School accommodated students from other small communities—such as, Hickory Plains, Des Arc, Hazen, DeValls Bluff, Upper Hill, and Brasfield—because there were no high schools in these small outlying towns.

During my eighth-grade year, our homeroom teacher, Ms. Odom, sold candy daily in order that we could take a field trip to Petit Jean Mountains, which is the homesite of former governor of Arkansas, Winthrop Rockefeller. We visited his farm on the mountain. His housetop and barn roof sparkled with crushed crystal rocks. What a beautiful sight to see as we drove into the farm. The sun was shinning on the rooftop, and it looked as though a trillion diamonds were sparkling atop his house and barns. It was an awesome sight to behold!

Ms. Odom knew Governor Rockefeller's caretaker, and he made sure we received the royal tour. The governor's barns were so cool. The space doubled for dances, barbecues, and political and entertaining functions.

For our high school senior trip, we visited Texarkana (at the Arkansas-Texas border) and Hot Springs. Our reservations were at the Arkansas Baptist Hotel. It was the only recognized hotel there, at that time, owned by blacks.

In Hot Springs, we observed spring waters spewing and steaming from the little natural fountains from the ground. Amazing!

Disciplinary problems at our school, as far as I could observe, were minimal. For one thing, parents would not hear of you going to school to get an education, (especially when this opportunity was not afforded most of them.) and receive a report from school that your child was acting out in any way or causing trouble. That just would not be the case. Teachers were allowed to use paddling as a deterrent to negative behavior. If your parents found out that any teacher had to deal with your negative behavior, you'd get it again at home. Because ours was a small town, everyone knew everyone else's business. It was understood if a neighbor or friend found your behavior in public unacceptable, it was okay for him or her to reprimand you verbally and give a report to your mother to boot! This is the true meaning of, "It takes a whole village to raise a child." Everyone was responsible for the entire community.

I remember my principal had to discipline some high school boys because they had been caught smoking and/or cursing, and he paddled them in front of our class. I guess it was to be an example to us all. My cousin Harvey Sanders was one of the group. He had some matches in his back pocket, and with the heated paddle to his behind, smoke began to billow from his pants. He was yelling, and everyone was excited and trying to put out the fire that started from the matches.

There were very few families with higher-educational expectations for their children. Parents didn't see college as an option for their kids. The best was to anticipate that most would finish high school. It would be a prideful moment for parents to see their son or daughter graduate and receive the education that they never received.

Surprisingly, more than just finishing high school was the end result, because many students moved away to better opportunities. Others went on to college. This truism remains constant: you can aspire to *do* whatever it is that you want to do or *be* whatever you want to be!

Augustine moved to New York, and then to California, with a promise to me that she would send for me on my graduation from high school. She stated that I could get a free college education there at one of the community colleges. Nevertheless, that never happened for me. All summer I waited to hear from her, as other friends and fellow students moved north to live with relatives and find a job or go on to college. I could not stand that summer was slowly slipping away and the thought of being left behind in this small town because there was nothing left for me to do in Biscoe.

As destiny would have it, my high school principal, Mr. McBeth, approached me to tell me in mid-August that he had a former classmate who had become the president of Shorter Junior College in North Little Rock, Arkansas, and he could get me in on a work-aid scholarship. (He did not ask me *if* I wanted to go to college but ... had high expectations for me to do it!) He made the call, and I was in.

Dr. H. Solomon Hill, the new president of Shorter College, offered me the position of his secretary. Woe! I was not worthy. He had information from my high school principal that my typing skills were good.

Doors began to open for me everywhere I went. All my needs were met, and desires were fulfilled that I didn't know that I had. How good is that? As destiny would have it, I decided that it was not for me to go to California to live with my sister after all.

*All things work together for the good ...*

College was the best time of my life. I didn't think that I had been properly prepared for the greatest milestone of my life, but I found that I blended quite well coming from a small farming town. The junior college setting was what I needed to make the initial adjustment to college life. Many likeminded students with similar background experiences made up the population at Shorter. Many kids came from small communities with some of the values that were imposed on me. I certainly do not regret that they had been imposed on me, because they helped me to build character using all the building blocks I needed for a successful life ahead of me.

Surrounded by friends at Shorter Jr. College in North Little Rock,

Jim and Blonzella Coleman, Terry Steppes, Annette Bullock, Robbie Duckworth, Reva Jones, Joyce Williams, Maxine Wynn, Sophia Tucker, Opal McBride, Costella Rudd, Cal Marie Perry, Lenora Chandler, Christine Tucker, Ligetta Rigsby, Emma Chidister, Bobby McGee, Leon Simpson, Sylvia Rutland, Richard Adams, Leon Martin, Melvin Caldwell, Betty Bridges, Welcome Talley, Big O, Della Jackson, Opal Preston, James Curlett, and so many more students from Shorter College helped me develop into the person that I am today. I believe that each person who came into my life at each milestone along the way helped to contribute to a specific need in me through divine design. The question might be, Did I pass the test?

I always remember that Scripture reminds me that in most cases, "It came to pass ..."

A few of the administrative staff were: Mrs. Hunter, our dorm matron; Mr. Young, our custodian (He always called me "Baby Face," which was an endearing way of making me feel special.); Mr. Griffin, our eloquent dean of students; our registrar; Ms. Hunter, and a very friendly and helpful staff of instructors that included, Mrs. Hill, Mr.

Harrell, Coach Goldsby, Mrs. Chandler, Mrs. Turner, Mrs. Sylvia de Peralto (from Brazil) and others.

College could have lasted a lifetime for me. It was a *perfect* time to be. I was born at the right time for every season of my life. There were many activities for me to participate in with other students. One of which surprised me when I was crowned Miss Freshman, and Dr. Ralph D. Abernathy just happened to pay a visit to our college and participated in the coronation. What sweet memories! What more could there be? I was soon to find out!

Money was short, but I made it work with the grace of God and the support of my mum. Once she sent me a package of paper-shell pecans from the large tree that grew in our front yard. At first, I was embarrassed because of the crudely wrapped packaging and the contents were none that I desired. However, I

knew that this was all that she had, and she was thinking of me. Another time, Mum sent me six dollars. Woe, I was so happy. I would make that six dollars last for quite a while. I knew that she had sold pecans or butter to get the money for me.

My high school experience had prepared me more than I knew for college and for my path in life. Home economics taught me how to sew, and I learned to design my own clothes for school. My own mum had been a good example of industrious ingenuity, and I learned from that. She knew how to make inadequate resources work to our advantage.

My brother Jesse, from Chicago, had come home for an extended visit, and he came by Shorter College to visit with me. He brought another few dollars and said that Mum had sold milk, eggs, and butter to be able to get the money for me.

I was surprised to have my stepfather visit me one surprising Sunday afternoon. He had taken the bus and then a cab to the campus with very little money in his pockets. I'm ashamed to say that I thought he would be an embarrassment to me because he was a drinker, and his educational background was somewhere around second or third grade. Nevertheless, he could hold a very intelligent conversation with the highest ranks. Life had been his educator. He talked with Mr. Harrell, my science teacher, sitting outside on a bench in front of the boy's dorm. I could see them from my dorm room. Mr. Harrell later told me that they had a great conversation together. I was proud of Homer. He had worn his crisp white shirt with his one and only black suit. He did look handsome. He was sober and very distinguished looking. I was sorry for having thought of him embarrassing me there. I so appreciated that he cared enough to come the distance and had shown a genuine interest in my well-being. He was like that. He did everything good for me. He was the only father that I had known.

I loved Shorter. I made good grades and good friends! The time that I spent there really anchored me. I learned a lot about life and all the basics of education that I should have received in high school. This experience could have lasted forever, but I needed to move on.

During my second year at Shorter, I married my friend and former high school typing teacher, James Holloway. He promised that if we got married, he would help me financially with my college tuition. I consented to marry him with the understanding that it was *not* a marriage of convenience.

Unfortunately, the first and only check that my new husband wrote for me—$125 to get back into school—*bounced*. I knew I was on my own again, after he repeatedly neglected to make the check good. I was embarrassed when I was called into the bursar's office. I applied for a student loan and was approved. It was the type of loan that carried a stipulation that if you pursued a teaching career and worked in a school teaching children of low socioeconomic status, 50 percent of the loan would be cancelled. Well, when I actually finished college and worked as a teacher for the next few years, my entire loan was canceled after making my initial payment on the loan, totaling around $188.

*Who was that?* My benefactor is and always has been my Father. Heavenly, that is.

I returned to college after taking a short leave to get married and later gave birth to our firstborn, Andre. I enrolled in Arkansas Mechanical and Normal College (A.M.&N.) at Pine Bluff, Arkansas, now known as the University of Arkansas at Pine Bluff (UAPB). I was still on track with students of the same age, because I had graduated high school at the age of fifteen. During my stay at A.M.&N. College, a couple of my friends told me that they had seen my name along with other students posted in the administration building on a notice stating that Dean Kyle wished to see us in his office. When I reported to his office, I was told that we would be taking a battery of tests for the North Central Accreditation Association Review Board, because the posted list of students had done well on previous tests. I remained on the Dean's List for the duration of time at A.M.&N. College, graduating cum laude in the summer of 1965.

My best buds at A. M. and N. College (UAPB) in Pine Bluff, Arkansas. Many nights were spent playing, "bid whist".

My new friends at A.M.&N. were Johnnie, Barbara, Willie, Irene, Anne, Lois, Carol, and many others. Our pastime was playing cards every night, attending rallies on campus, going roller skating, attending activities at the Student Union, and so many other clean, fun things was available for us to do. We just liked hanging out together. That was fun in and of itself! Sometimes my friends and I would play cards so late into the night that I would have to get up at three or four o'clock in the morning to study.

It worked for me! I never failed a class. In fact, I remained on the honor roll every semester.

I also matriculated at State College of Arkansas in Jonesboro, the summer of 1967, taking coursework in library science in preparation for my position at DeValls Bluff Elementary School.

# My Career Development

Developmentally, my career in education began before I even received my bachelor's degree. While I was between marriage and a college break, I accepted a job as a teacher in Forest City, Arkansas. It was from January until May. This school district had a worse record of student attendance because of child labor than ours at Biscoe. Little children were just beginning school in January because of cotton-harvesting season. It was really a sad situation. At least I knew my alphabet, how to count, and could read when I began first grade. These first-graders did not even know their alphabet or numbers this late in the school year. I wish that I had had the foresight and an angered passion to do whatever it would have taken to bring change to the way children were exploited for landlord's gain. At the end of that school year, I went back to college to finish my education.

I moved to Gary, Indiana, in September of 1969 and immediately enrolled at Indiana University Northwest campus in Gary to begin coursework for my master's degree, as I had accepted a job in the Gary Community School Corporation. I was awarded my master of science degree in the summer of 1975. I considered this trek to Indiana a divine move that took me on a course fulfilling my career in teaching that expanded over thirty-eight years. I loved teaching because I love children, and it is always my desire to help elevate the level of educational consciousness in our youth.

This journey has afforded me opportunities for personal and professional advancement. Personally, I have had many options to explore the world outside my chosen profession of teaching. Hence, I engaged myself in many exploits in entrepreneurship. I attempted cosmetics sales through house parties; presented artistic works to my friends, family, and acquaintances; offered private showings of household products; along with embracing many other avenues to bring money into the home and to expand my ability to cross over into experiencing the work habits of the other side.

The most interesting exploit would have been my investing part of my savings in stock in People's Beer Company, a brewery based in Oshkosh, Wisconsin. The brewery was bombed when the trucks began rolling and were well on their way to make us, the investors, millionaires. Because of the bombing, I had a delay in reaching my goal of becoming a millionaire.

When all else fails, we must pick ourselves up again and begin looking forward to *what could be* rather than *what could have been*.

Often when one door closes, I have learned that there is another door ready to open for me. Thank God, He has always been there for me.

Early in my teaching career and at our school district's sponsorship, I, along with three other colleagues, visited the Dade County Schools in Florida to observe how federally funded Chapter I (Title I) was implemented and its ramifications for our district.

Sometime later, I decided to apply, at our school's invitation, to receive training through Meca-Seton Montessori Center, in Hinsdale,

Illinois, in the Pre-primary discipline. This training would enable me to work with pre-kindergarten children at Bethune Early Childhood Education using the Montessori method of teaching. Marie Montessori's philosophy of education gave me a greater perceptive in educational strategies and methodology. Our pre-kindergarten center was/is the only one of its magnitude and kind in the state of Indiana.

Each level of advancement toward my career goals catapulted me effortlessly to goals attained. In fact, I never knew what my goals would be from one milestone to another. The way seemed to be already set for me, and I just followed the path. Someone has said, "It is not the destination but the journey that counts." I really do identify with this quote. I wouldn't take anything for the journeys that I have had. It seemed everyone I met and everything I did had a purpose in shaping my personality and ultimately, my destiny.

In 1994, I traveled to five cities in China through sponsorship of People to People, the Eisenhower Endowment Foundation, to participate in observations and discussions on "Play in Education," I was again privileged to attend at the expense of our school district.

Yet again in 1996, I was blessed to be a part of a cadre of teachers from Gary (Jacky Gholson, Claire Chube, Willie Arnold, Helen Rogers, and myself ), as well as professionals across the nation, led by Dr. Molefi Asante, to travel to six villages in Ghana, West Africa. The purpose of this trip was to exchange cultures, traditions, and to infuse African American studies into all of our schools in the district. The next infusion process was to complete coursework in the Harlem Renaissance from the African-American Studies Department through Indiana University Northwest campus.

A very lasting relationship developed between my African sister, Mary Ohemeng, and I. She was a kindergarten teacher at the Crig Primary School in New Tafo, Akin, in Ghana. I resolved in my heart that when I returned home, I would send supplies and materials to help her and her class. Mary has since opened a school herself; she has a great passion for helping children. Monetary donations, school supplies, and educational electronic games and toys are continually sent to her with many of my colleagues helping the cause.

Sponsorship has been a door of opportunity for me to bless several children in South America, Asia, and Africa through World Vision and the Christian Children's Fund. These offerings to help others have realized manifold blessings for my children and me.

*Charity begins at home.*

Children have always been in my head and in my heart. I have an anointing for children abroad as well as here at home. I can't begin to tell all the ways I have opted to help children. My most fun way was to "adopt" a child each year at the school where I taught so that I could help them in some way. Mentoring is a great way to encourage and motivate children. It gives opportunities to meet parents, become a positive role model, provide guided assistance, and in some small way provide for tangible needs to the family.

Teaching is so rewarding! Over the years, more children have caused me to laugh more than to cry. I remember Toni. Toni was a frisky little second-grader who said uncanny things that brought a smile to my mouth. On one particular morning, I had been rushing to get to school in a timely manner, and I had eaten my breakfast, an orange, on the run. Toni was sitting close to me in the reading group, and she said, "I smell orange." To this, I replied, "That's because I had an orange on my way to work this morning." Then she said, "Oh, I didn't know that you worked!"

Blended with all these experiences, our family has shared cultures with five foreign exchange students from Belgium, France, Colombia, Germany, and Brazil, as well as three exchange teachers from Japan and three students from Israel during their visit to the United Stated promoting worldwide relationships and touring with the Tnuatron Dance Group.

Intermingled with work was always an opportunity to play. Indiana University Northwest Campus had a great connection with community to invite participation in its annual performing arts events. I decided to try out for a spring production of Cole Porter's *Anything Goes*. This was so much fun. It was far greater than performing in elementary school plays as a child. I had a dual role as many of the actors and actresses. I was trained well by Mr. Garrett Cope, our producer and director, to be one of the dancers.

It was always my desire to do all the things that I thought I wanted to do while on this earth. I desired to be versatile in work and play. I wanted to develop a résumé of life that spoke of fulfillment and realization. God had given me this profound gift of life, and I was bound to live it to my fullest attempt in order to bring Him glory.

I wanted to advocate for children. This led me to establish a Children's Advocate Center. I wanted to help children who were mainly victims of physical and mental abuse. I was inspired by a trip to Washington, D.C., where Marian Wright-Edelman engaged tens of thousands of people from all over the nation to Stand for Children under the umbrella of the Children's Defense Fund. I came away with a greater commitment to help children develop their greatest potential. I opened the Children's Advocate Center as a child-care center in 1997.

I also attended training through the Porter County court system to learn how to advocate for victims' rights. I received technology training at Valparaiso High School in the evenings when I realized that schools would be logging onto the information superhighway, and I did not want to be left behind. My thirst for knowledge was also evident when I thought I needed to prepare myself for securing properties that came up in county, about three plots, one of which was a nice, four-unit commercial property. I share ownership of this property with Eileen, my friend and former co-worker.

It was not a difficult decision for me to obtain my administrative license in education during my sabbatical leave in years 1999 and 2000. I was able to study under Dr. Vernon G. Smith, who was a former principal at Nobel School, and now my professor at Indiana University NW. I also gleaned from Dr. Lucille Washington and Dr. Becky Hollaway while working as a Title I facilitator to develop a program of achievement for our elementary students. I decided to use my administrative license in the manner for which I had earned it.

I retired after working the last two years of my career as principal of Bethune Early Childhood Development Center. It was now time to begin a new day of a new season in my life.

# Reflections

*The Word in me, Works for Me!*

Classified as second-class citizens, child-labor injustices, inequalities in the educational system, and economical deprivation have continued a perpetuation of the enslavement of the mind, soul, and spirit for a race of people already fraught from decades of slavery. We still dream, and we still rise!

I never dreamed that, as a child thinking about *"how awesome"* Ms. Odom was as a teacher and landowner, I would rise to that level and even surpass her in many ways. She was the measuring stick for my life. If she could do it as a single black woman, then what was stopping me? I suppose that she had a favorable edge on me because her parents could have benefited from post-Reconstruction opportunities. Besides which, some of her characteristic traits dictated she possibly had an advantage colorwise.

Since our mum had a profound trust and dependence on God as our source, we were more than *survivors*, we were *overcomers* and *victorious* in all things. She was an example of undaunting faith, untiring ways, and standing for what one believes in. I believe that we, as her children, reaped the residual consequence of her prayers even until this day. Had it not been for the grace and mercy of God, I would have a different story to tell. But because of Him, we didn't just survive, we lived!

Dr. Spock authored a book in the early '60s on child care that changed decades of raising children. I believe children were being given too much liberality in decision-making issues during the '60s and '70s. We're seeing the backlash of these principles today. These liberalities, in essence, release parents from a sense of responsibility in the guidance and protection of their child. Parents need always set limits and direct their children until they are able to make responsible decisions about their own lives. Building a solid foundation should be predicated on parents' positive impartations into their child's life.

Children are not able call on life's experiences to know wisdom in all things. Wisdom in its fullest is distributed with the passing of time.

*Wisdom is the principal thing, therefore get wisdom.*

Mr. McBeth, my high school principal, defined "wisdom" as something like this: "Wisdom is knowing when/how to act, and when/what/how to speak, at a given time."

Parents are always role models for their children. Like it or not, we represent! We're not going to be perfect parents. I wasn't. Life's experiences bring *patience and understanding*. It would be good to have it early on, but we know that the *journey* is always before the *destination*! The great thing is to prepare for the journey by gaining the proper knowledge for empowerment in your chosen station in life. Prepare your children through training and exposure to intangible lessons in life. As simple as it may seem, create areas of interest to maintain personal balance for your children, such as, piano, swim, little sports, gymnastics, create creative platforms, or other children.

Become involved in school projects, volunteer at your child's school, be visible in community and school activities. Set boundaries, limits, and rules early in your child's life. Believe me, they will later appreciate you for it. Be the parent and no so much the friend.

*Train up a child in the way that he should go and he will not depart from it.*

Our nation's children are in peril. How will we reach them? They deserve responsible parenting, phenomenal teachers, great role models, and the setting of boundaries. We've tried reaching them physically, mentally, morally, and intellectually with little benefit. The greatest appeal would be to their souls.

I've always been told to, "Do unto others as you would have them do unto you," which many claim is the Golden Rule of life. As you purpose in your heart to help others, know that you have made a contribution to the bank of life, and it enables you to make a withdrawal greater than your deposit.

Acts of kindness take me back as far as a time when my friend Mae Bertha gave me a coloring book that must have cost all of five cents. I treasured that coloring book and loved using the crayons that smelled so fruity and nice. I must have been about nine years old. Mae Bertha taught me how to color within the lines and personalize my colorings by adding designs into the pictures, such as flowers in the little girl's dresses, stripes in the shirts, and shades of skin colorings. She was very good at neatness and creating great design in her work. Something as small as this impressed me for a lifetime. It was the idea of giving to others with the chance that the receiver would continue this contagious act of caring for others.

*Give and it shall be given unto you, good measure.*

The principles that are taught to one generation will yield a much different result from that of another. There are many extenuating circumstances that may affect the results. Sometimes a generation is skipped when the mores of a society's behaviors flow from positive to a dominated negative. These behaviors become much too acceptable through being caught up in the influence of bad lyrics in music, immorality, sinfulness, and spiritual lack in the home.

We embrace, applaud, and believe that we have a new hope in President Barack Obama. Let us not even think for a moment that President Obama will be able to solve all of this nation's ills by himself. Given his openness to the Spirit of God for wisdom, God will empower President Obama with the ability to solve the monumental problems we face and bring into fruition the necessary change to move our country forward.

Can we afford to sit back and see if he can do it? We cannot! Every citizen has a responsibility to do all that is necessary to ensure that the plan involves all of us working together. God can and will move the right persons into position in order to make great things happen. He has been waiting for us to yield to Him and through divine might, will, provocation, and power, he is able to "heal the land."

Who is He, who has presented to us a virtually unknown who is able to connect with all races because of his heritage? My God, who is able to make all grace abound for us all, blesses whom He will bless, brings promotion to the humble, and sends Obama into our midst to lead this nation, "for such a time as this." Because of Obama's heritage, he is able to walk among all races and nationalities of peoples.

It had already been prophesied that Barack Obama would be the *chosen* to lead the nation for this period in time. He is a vessel ready to be used. His very name suggests *kinship* with God. Now is the *appointed* time. It is our opportunity to prove to the whole world that we can stand together with our president to unify our country and make envious all the nations of the world by our example.

Peace can become a reality in Jerusalem, rest can be realized where there is unrest, help is available and shall give to the helpless, differences of races and nationalities can be respected, and maybe the word of God that is required of us, "Love one another," will become revelation to everyone.

Much can be said of the experiences that contributed to my becoming the person that I am today. My story does not end here, for I still have miles to go before I'm done. There are still dreams to be fulfilled and a destiny to realize. I am convinced that I must live and not die that I may declare the Glory of God in my lifetime. There are many territories that are unchartered, vast mountaintops that have never been climbed, and so many souls waiting to be won.

There is never a time when I can say, "I am there!" Money or possessions cannot answer the call. What defines us is our *service* and *love* toward our fellow people. Our arms are not too short that we cannot reach out and touch in some small way the hearts and souls of others.

We never know how others are impacted by the smallest or insignificant deeds that we perform for them. These deeds are often multiplied resulting in a sum that is greater than all of its parts. For example, right after graduating from college, I was employed for a year and a half at Biscoe Elementary School (formerly known as Prairie County Training School), which I had attended as a child. It was my delight to celebrate Christmas with my class by sharing treats and small gifts with them. In 2005, while on my way to my alma mater at UAPB for our annual homecoming in Pine Bluff, Arkansas, I stopped through my little hometown. As I turned off US Highway 70, I began to reflect on days long past. I drove slowly through the street leading into town and observed a young man on a bicycle who had stopped and was looking my way. I noticed that he had more than several gray strands of hair on his head. I pulled over next to him and spoke with him momentarily. I introduced myself. He looked familiar. He stated that he knew who I was and let me know *how* he knew me so well! He said, "You made Christmas for us when I was in your class." That had been over thirty-eight years ago!

This is how I had been remembered. Perhaps that was the most important thing for him to remember about me. I predicted that he might have said, "You taught me how to read," or, "I learned so much from you being my teacher." We cannot predict what others will hold onto given the chance that we may say a word, plant a seed, or perform a deed on their behalf. Anyhow, his words were touching and far reaching, and I'll always remember to allow myself to be open to the greatest gift. For me, that is giving.

Giving is not only of tangible things but of things that would uplift mankind through encouragement and inspiration.

To attest to some of the returns of giving even of your time and talents in the teaching profession, is that children remember the good in you for years to come and will occasionally find reasons to acknowledge the good they see in you in some way. Audrey Donaldson was a very scholarly and unpretentious student in my fifth-grade class at Nobel School. When she was a senior in high school, she nominated me for *Who's Who* among America's teachers. For me, it was an honor to receive this validation as being a good teacher and that she *chose* to pay tribute to me.

Many people have inspired me with a desire to help others: my mum; my former pastor, Elder W. J. Johnson; my present bishop, Arthur Braizer; my high school principal, Mr. McBeth; Dr. H. Solomon Hill, Prexy of Shorter College '61; Dr. Vernon G. Smith; Dr. Mildred C. Harris, my spiritual sister in the Lord; Joyce Meyer; Joel Osteen and

Kenneth Hagin, TV evangelists; UNICEF; Feed the Children sponsors; National Defense Children's founder, Marian Edelman-Wright; Bono; the Bill and Melinda Gates Foundation; Nelson Rockefeller; and especially Ms. TV personality herself, Oprah Winfrey, to just name a few. We don't have to look very far to find great people who inspire us to love our neighbor as ourselves.

*Goodness begets goodness!*

We are put on this earth to help one another. During a TV broadcast, Joel Osteen (Lakewood Church, Houston, Texas) acknowledged that a child said, "When we help each other out, that's what being civilized means."

The greatest lesson in life that I have learned for myself, after the lesson of love, is the lesson to *forgive*. Forgiveness releases our debts and our debtors. It paves the way for *our* blessings to flow; it frees us from bondage and energizes us to hope, dream, and realize our destiny. Forgiveness is a matter of choice. One must choose to forgive no matter the hurt or anger.

Life is a mystery! The more we uncover the little mysteries of life, the more we are able to live and not just exist. Life keeps us vibrant, interested, anticipating, and going back to the square to begin again and get it right.

I would be remiss if I didn't share with others what I have learned through experiencing the goodness of God and what He has done for me. The Bible states that "God will lead us, and guide us through all paths," and certainly He has done that for me. If everything were left up to me to order my own steps, I'd mess up royally! Sure, I have challenges and problems that I encounter, but that is necessary for me to know that I have a God who can help me solve them.

*Goodness and mercy shall follow me all the days of my life.*

I love the promises of God. Knowledge is a good thing to have! To know that God says, "Fear not, little flock it is my good pleasure to give you the kingdom."

How precious is that! Or "Seek first, the kingdom of God and His righteousness, and all these things shall be added unto you." One of the first Scriptures that I learned as a child was, "The Lord is my shepherd, I shall not want." However, the very first one was, "Jesus wept."

# Epilogue

*Now go and live life to the fullest.* Don't give up, because as you've heard, "Nothing beats a failure but a try!" And, "There's a better day ahead." "Every new day is a new beginning to wipe the slate clean and start *anew.*" You will never know what great things await you at the next junction if you throw up your hands and say, "Forget it!" Many have lost out because they fell down and stayed down.

The army has a great slogan, "Be all that you can be." The slogan does not intimate that you need a good running start in order "to be"; neither does it imply that you need a perfect background in order "to be." All you need to do is "be." Nike's slogan is, "Just do it!" What are you waiting for? *Life Is a Story.* What is your story?

# A Poem of Freedom

By Ernestine May

1961

Dedicated to the Memory of Dr. H. Solomon Hill, Former president of Shorter Jr. College.

*(Written my freshman year at Shorter Jr. College and edited for publication.)*

Freedom is free,
For you, but not me;
Free as the birds,
Just only one word ...
To choose where you live
To share and to give,
Free to be free,

Why can't it be me?
Free to worship,
Serve God and hear the Bishop,
Free to be me.
Let every Black man stand up and declare—

Let Freedom Ring,
Let the birds of the air sing.
Freedom is here and should be seen!
Looking back, can't you see?
It's time for us to be free.
When years of oppression are no more,
From the dungeons of Africa to our shining shore,
Shackled and sold,
Many stories untold.
Hanged, tortured and cheated of life,
Living a lifetime at the hands of strife.
Who will come to rescue my people?
It was a time to abolish, and Lincoln looked deeper!
Anticipation—as we wait for the time,
Slavery was the White man's crime.
Freedmen found it hard to be free,
They were sometimes found hanging from a tree.
Shackled of mind, in
God's grace we find,

In our journey of hope we are inclined,
Of an identity of blackness defined!
Emancipation, proclamation,
Civil unrest,
Separation, hesitation,
Pass the White man's test.

Marches, demonstrations, Nonviolent sit-ins,
Trying our best,
There is a ring, another King who says freedom is not far,
Stay the course. It's not yet time to cross that bar!

THE END

LaVergne, TN USA
20 January 2010
170659LV00002B/2/P